Depression DOESN'T Discriminate

Sophia Manarolis

Disclaimer: This book is certainly not for the faint-hearted, and it's filled with triggers! The content of "Depression DOESN'T Discriminate" is for informational purposes only and is not intended to diagnose, treat, or cure any condition or disease. This is a vivid, raw and unfiltered recounting of my personal experiences with depression, including some graphic details about some of my attempts to end my own life. If you're on the verge of suicide like I've been, my hope is that this book will convince you that your life matters. If you're in the middle of a suicide crisis, put this book down for now and Google search the suicide crisis helpline of your country, and call them STAT...because YOU MATTER! If your country is not listed anywhere on Google, please contact your local emergency services, or reach out to someone you love to help you do so! **REMEMBER: Your Life Matters!!!**

Published by: Motivation and Success Publishing
The publisher is not responsible for websites (or their content) that are not owned by the publisher.

Paperback ISBN 13: 979-8-9885854-4-2
Hardcover ISBN-13: 979-8-9885854-5-9
Printed in the United States of America.

This book is dedicated to those who have been there during the major depressive episodes that took over my life, especially those who stuck around and never gave up on me. You know who you are.

I am eternally grateful to you.

With much love,

Sophs

Testimonials

"I was going to download the chapter and read it later today but after taking a quick peek at the first couple of sentences, I found myself reading until the end of the chapter. Wow Sophia! The way you bring the reader along through a very dark moment in your life is gripping, gut-wrenching, raw and, dare I say it, uncomfortable. And that's exactly what we all need in order to understand the struggles of someone's battle with depression and suicide. Thank you for sharing with the world your most vulnerable moments and I look forward to reading the entire book. We all need to gain a better understanding of depression and how it can affect us and our loved ones. Getting your "inside view" of what it feels like when your mind is not "home" is something we ALL need to understand in order to break the mental health stigma and drive change. It's about time somebody wrote like this!"

—Lia Gribilas

"I was reading your story and I was picturing you. I can't explain it. You usually imagine characters. I just... I can't find the words. I'm not going to lie though, when I got to the part about you mom, now being a mother I literally almost broke down. How helpless a parent feels when such a monster has taken over their child's mind and you can't do anything. I know the story isn't just based on that but it got me really choked up. The saying goes 'I'm hoping my story touches at least one person'. I believe your story will hit many, and I'm happy that you're around to tell it."

—Georgia Makrigiannis

"Wow!! OMG, that 1st chapter captivated me and I wanted to read the entire book in one sitting! Just the fact I know you and your family brought chills down my spine! God bless you and your movement!"

—Dino M.

"I was putting off reading Chapter 1, I wasn't sure if I wanted to read it. In the end, I read every line with goosebumps all over my body and tears rolling down my face. So glad that dreadful day wasn't your last!!! So glad your angels were there for you!! God bless you!"

—Voula Karnezis

"Powerful. Raw. Real. No "filter". These are just some of the adjectives that come to mind when reading Chapter 1. I was truly blown away. I just couldn't put it down, it's like I was transported right there with you and had a much better understanding of that monster, that all-encompassing invisible demon that could infect someone's life and who's just as deadly as his cousin cancer! It takes a tremendous amount of courage and strength to unveil yourself like this, so publicly. You are sincerely inspirational and I have no doubt this will help so so so many people out there. Thank you from the bottom of my heart. #grateful"

—Theo Giovanis

"Wow Sophia…just phenomenal! Chapter 1 is so well written and very detailed...bringing us along in your deepest thoughts. You got my attention and will get every reader's attention no doubt. This book will help many! I cried...I felt your pain and that of your mom. I wish you nothing but continued success stories from now. Thank you for continuing to raise awareness. I can't wait to read the rest of the book!!"

—Roula Vrentzos

"Riveting!!! Keeps you wanting to know more, to know your story, to understand how these demons work. The end narrative will be phenomenal and will be a useful tool for many to comprehend and help others suffering from this illness!"

—Lemonia Strapatsas

"Your vulnerability is commendable Sophia... Through it I hope you not only are able to help others, shed some light, and bring even more awareness to this terrible monster but that you also find peace."

—Eleni Papakonstantinou

"I read Chapter 1, and oh my God what can I say? Do I start with the physical effect it had on my body...mental or emotional ? I felt every single word you wrote... My breaking point (when the tears began) was your mother. God bless you for being alive, for sharing your story, for your courage, for everything."

—Irene S.

"Sophia, I read the first chapter of your book and all I have to say is you are such a remarkable woman. You talk about this demon in you that tried to make you hurt yourself, but you overcame it. I just wanted to read more and more of your book as I was reading chapter 1. And yes, I cried when reading what you were going through. Love you."

—Despina Bourdaras

"Just finished reading Chapter 1, and I can't stop crying. I need time to register it all. This was raw and scary. You had told me about your episodes but reading this made it all so real… I am still crying as I write this. Your book will help a lot of people."

—Penny Chatzinas

"I got a chance to read the first chapter. It flowed so well, and knowing you and your story, I couldn't stop reading. There was a reason you did not die that day. Your purpose in life is not over! Keep on helping those in need that might be going through the same thing. There are many people who love you and care about you including me."

—Helen Mentzelos

"Sophia, I just read the first chapter and all I can say is WOW! I was right there with you feeling all of the emotions of every person included. I have never attempted to take my life but there have been times I felt like that would be an option to consider. Your book is so needed in the world. I am so glad there was an army of God's angels watching over you so you can bring this important message to a world that so needs it. I see you on talk shows, stages and even schools sharing your message to encourage others and give them HOPE! You ROCK my friend. I am so incredibly blessed to know you."

—Sandie Grindel

"Depression Doesn't Discriminate is real, raw, and intense. Sophia holds nothing back as she candidly shares her honest, most vulnerable and revealing truth about what it's really like living with depression. Sophia is bringing so much light into the world with this book. I believe this book will be a lighthouse for many people living with depression and for those who love them. Not only will it change the way we look at depression, and open our eyes, but it will also equip us with tools we need to fight and win!"

—Lindy Lewis

Table of Contents

Testimonials 7

Table of Contents 15

Foreword 19

Prologue 23

Chapter 1—You'll Never Understand Me 29

Chapter 2—"Mom, I Have A Problem" 41

Chapter 3—"I'm Really Scared, T. I Don't Wanna Die" 59

Chapter 4—Humanity: 1. The *Monster*: 0 81

Chapter 5—"If You Do This Again, You WILL Kill
        Him" 109

Chapter 6—The Decarie Expressway 125

Chapter 7—"But What Did John 3:16 Really Say?" 147

Chapter 8—What Tony Has to Say About the Original
        3:16 Day 167

Chapter 9—When History Repeats Itself 189

Epilogue 215

About The Author 219

To the fifty of you who preordered my book while I was in the process of writing it, I am forever grateful for the encouragement your gesture provided. Writing this book was no small feat, as a lot of unhealed trauma was unearthed. Good news is—GREAT news, actually—I did some next-level healing during this process, and I'm very much looking forward to writing Part 2, *The Monster Strikes Back.*

To anyone else who has purchased this book ever since its release, THANK YOU for helping me grow the I'M ALIVE Movement and normalizing the conversation surrounding burnout, depression, and suicide.

"Alone we can do so little; together we can do so much."

—Helen Keller

Stay tuned …

Foreword

Depression Doesn't Discriminate is a vital resource for anyone looking to better understand this complex and often misunderstood condition. Sophia's heartfelt and vulnerable personal recounting of her experiences battling depression is eye-opening and impactful. Her expertise on this subject shines through in each chapter, providing readers with a deeper understanding and perspective of the impact of depression on suicide survivors and those currently suffering.

One of the most significant contributions of this book is the way it encourages a more open dialogue about the effects of depression and breaks down the stigma and shame often associated with mental illness. Sophia creates a safe space for readers to explore their own experiences and emotions through her magnetic storytelling. This is especially important for suicide survivors, who may feel isolated and alone in their grief.

This book not only offers powerful insights but also practical strategies to help identify, recognize and manage symptoms. Sophia offers valuable resources for finding support, which may be lifesaving for those struggling with depression.

This book is a must-read for anyone looking to improve their own mental health or to support a loved one who is struggling. It offers hope and guidance for a brighter future and a powerful call to action for more open and honest conversations about depression so that more lives can be saved through The I'M ALIVE Movement (#its316andimalive).

Let's link arms as a global collective in helping normalize the conversation and to get this book on every coffee table around the world!

Stronger Together,

Charlene Helm and Noelle McGough, The Challenge Queens

Hosts: *The Become Revolutionary Show & Podcast*

Prologue

There's Always H.O.P.E.

Four major depressive episodes and a few suicide attempts later, my life's purpose has been and continues to be to **H**elp **O**pen **P**eople's **E**yes about their own mental health and the potential for it to go to shit because, guess what?

Depression DOESN'T discriminate.

It can happen to every person reading this book right now, no matter your gender, age, sex, race, class, religion, ethnicity, ability, language, sexual orientation, or relationship status. Essentially, it can happen to anyone on the planet—including **you.**

Take it from me … I was once a first-year university student with no history of depression or suicidal ideation (in myself or in my family), just a history of applying *way* too much pressure on myself to succeed—something that today I call unnecessary suffering.

That year, at age eighteen, I had the first of many major depressive episodes. It lasted six months. It was debilitating enough for me to have to pause and withdraw from my studies midway through my first semester, after having busted my butt to ace those midterms. This was the first time I had ever experienced such mental torment and the first time thoughts of self-harm had ever entered my mind.

Here's the thing most people don't know: If you have lived with major depression, you become susceptible to

25

experiencing it again—a fact I seemed to have skipped over when studying for my psychology-related midterms and something that is not really talked about in society.[1]

So, six and a half years after recovering from major depression, just before entering the last semester of my master's program, it happened again.

And guess what? I recovered from that episode six months later. Six months after that, after having gone back to university to complete my master's, it happened AGAIN! This time, though, things got a lot scarier, and on March 16, 2011, I tried to die.

I repeat:

Depression DOESN'T discriminate.

Anyone, no matter how successful they may seem, *can* be affected!

Many who have considered suicide didn't really want to die; they simply wanted the pain to stop. Suicide, though, is **not** the answer. Getting the right help *is*.

The day I tried to die will never escape my mind and has officially become the most important day of my life ... what I now call *3:16 Day* (third month, sixteenth day). It is the day I was given a second chance to live—to stick around to appreciate one of the greatest gifts I have ever been given: LIFE.

---

[1] https://www.ncbi.nlm.nih.gov/pmc/articles/PMC2169519/

Somewhere along the way, I fell back into the trap of living as an immortal, and six years after recovering from that near-death experience, a lack of self-love and proper self-care led me into the worst major depressive episode yet. That thirteen-month period, which nearly killed me more times than I can count on my fingers, began one month after returning from my beautiful honeymoon. It led me to shut down my private practice that I had worked so hard to build over the years. Again:

Depression DOESN'T discriminate.

Anyone and everyone, no matter how happy they have been and how many major positive life transitions they've walked through, can be affected.

As Tony Robbins, a well-known life coach I truly admire, has said at many of his transformative events, "If you can find grace within yourself from your worst experience, then maybe your worst experience has become your best." I know that's the case for me as I have managed to transform my struggles with mental illness and attempted suicide into a movement of gratitude and hope—the I'M ALIVE Movement.

#its316andimalive, its316andimalive.com

In this book, you will read my story about what it is like to live with this *monster* known as depression. You'll learn what can really go through the mind of someone attempting to end their own life and how you can help someone you love suffering from depression. Because this book serves as an exact recording of my thoughts during several major depressive episodes, some verbiage used contradicts inclusive, person-first language. While I have reported here that the monster in my head used the word "retarded," it is not a word I condone. It is often used as a derogatory term to insult and demean individuals with intellectual or developmental disabilities, and I do NOT approve of this type of language or its harmful effects. If this word is something you continue to use today, I kindly ask that moving forward, you join many of us in spreading kindness and understanding, creating a more inclusive and respectful world for all, and substituting it with "person with an intellectual disability."

Hopefully, this book will also inspire you to take better care of your own mental health.

"Your mental health is everything—prioritize it. Make the time like your life depends on it, because it does."

—Mel Robbins[2]

---

[2] https://twitter.com/melrobbins/status/1063802729691267073?lang=en

Chapter 1

You'll Never Understand Me

Wednesday, March 16, 2011
(3/16/2011)

"Meet me at the store at noon. We're going to see Dr. Farquhar today."

Here we go. Another message from my brother. There's no way that's going to happen. I've done this before—I've been here before.

Anxiety flared through my body like fire.

Dr. Farquhar is great, but I saw him during the last episode. I can't do that again. There is no way I am going back to a psych ward. I'd rather die than go back there. I am done. This kind of life is simply not worth living. Today is the day I put an end to all this suffering.

I slowly rose from my best friend Olga's bed, grabbed my purse, and looked to make sure the bottle of Tylenol and pack of Gravol I'd purchased a couple days ago were in there.

It's too bad Olga's at work. I would love to hug her one last time ... and say goodbye.

I saw Dr. Farquhar, a psychiatrist at the Douglas Mental Health Hospital, during a second major depressive episode. At that time, the *monster* known as depression had me convinced that I was mildly intellectually disabled. That's right, me—the person who had officially completed her master's degree in counselling at the University of Ottawa—strongly believed I was mildly intellectually disabled.

According to many psychiatrists I had spoken to, this was impossible. No matter how much I tried to convince them of how badly I suffered from mental challenges, they were adamant that an intellectual disability was impossible because not only had I made it into a graduate program, but I'd aced all my graduate work.

Yet after several trips to the psychiatric emergency room and having completed an eight-week outpatient program, I was convinced my intellectual disability wasn't being recognized, and I'd had enough of being misunderstood.

I am mentally retarded,[3] not mentally ill. Everyone at the Douglas is mentally ill, so I don't belong with them there. There's no fuckin' way I'm going back.

I've got to find a place to disappear to. A place where I can swallow these pills and not be found while they take time to kick in.

Hmmmmm ... Where do I go?

My brother's expecting me at the store, though. Fuck.

I left Olga's apartment with no idea what would happen next. I was so anxious, my body felt like it was burning. My thoughts were racing and irrational. I messaged my brother Tony.

"I'm on my way, but I really don't want to go back to the Douglas. Please don't take me there. Please."

---

[3] See prologue

"We'll discuss this when you get here. Just get here for noon."

Olga lived about twenty minutes from my parents' store on Park Avenue and Bernard Street. That short drive was excruciating. I screamed, hyperventilated, and wept intensely. Anxiety had gotten the best of me.

I was so afraid of what I had decided to do. Did I really want to die? Did I? I still wasn't sure.

In retrospect, it's easier to say that what I wanted was to no longer live this way. I wanted the mental torment to end. But at that moment, the *monster* had definitely convinced me that putting an end to my own life was not only the best solution—it was the ONLY solution.

The goal was absolutely to die that day.

So off I went, in the direction of my parents' store, turning onto streets that wouldn't directly lead me there. I went through my old neighborhood and considered parking in a family friend's driveway. I knew they were in Dubai and wouldn't be back in town for at least three months. There was no chance anyone would pass by their home on that day or at least a couple days that followed, which is all I would need to ensure I made this work.

So I pulled in.

But how will this make them feel—knowing I ended my life while parked at their home?

Will this cause any kind of trauma?

Is that fair to them?

Is that how I want them to remember me? As selfish, not considering how it would make them feel to have something like this associated with their home?

Fuck it. Find somewhere else in Outremont to do this.

The twenty minutes my brother had given me had long passed, and he texted, asking me where I was. I ignored the texts, driving in circles not too far from him … trying to find that special spot where I could park my car and go unnoticed for some time.

He proceeded to call. I flushed the call and, within minutes, shut off my phone. As I drove up and down Mont-Royal, Tony called 911 to file a missing person's report, even though I hadn't really gone missing … yet. He begged and pleaded with the police to start the process because he knew I was suicidal—a major reason he wanted me to see Dr. Farquhar at noon.

Fortunately for all of us, the police took my brother seriously and filed a report. My brother then called my family and friends, even those across the border, in case I had driven into New York state and contacted them. Part of Tony was hanging on to the idea that all I wanted was to get away from him and be left alone for a little while.

I continued to drive, thoughts racing a million miles an hour.

Am I allowed to park here? Will a meter attendant approach my car? I'm not sure how long it will take for this bottle of Tylenol to kick in. It could take hours before my organs stop functioning. I gotta make sure I don't get interrupted ...

Is this a side of the street where the snow removal crew will pass? What is today? Wednesday? Do they clean the snow on the right or the left side in the Plateau? It's on the right side. I should be good here.

Are my back windows tinted enough so I don't get spotted? Is this park for children or for pet owners? It's too cold for anyone to go to the park today, anyway! I think I'm good. Going to park my truck and make sure no one notices me getting into my back seat.

My anxiety had reached new heights, and because I'd read about suicide several times in the last couple days, I knew that people had a tendency to back down when the time came to swallow all those pills. I used whatever techniques I had to pump myself up to get something done. And, of course, the *monster* didn't hesitate to assist in the process.

You got this, Sophs. You got this.
You got this!
You can do this! Yes, you can!
This is for the best! You will no longer be a burden. No one will have to deal with you or take care of you anymore! You have to do this.
You have to!
For their sake and yours.
Do it.
Just do it!
One by one.

Let's go!
One more!
Don't stop.
Keep going.
One more.
Just keep swallowing!
This has to be done.
It's for the best.
Keep going!
One more.
You got this.
You can do this.
Almost there.
Just a couple more!
You got this!
You did it!
Where's the Gravol™?
Take the Gravol™ now!

After swallowing fifty extra-strength Tylenol at warp speed, I took several Gravol™, a doctor-recommended treatment for nausea and vomiting, to ensure I did not throw up all that I had just ingested.

Then I waited.

I waited to die, hoping it wouldn't be a slow and painful death.

I had read on suicide-related forums (yes, those exist) that once one major organ shuts down, it isn't long before the rest follow.

The *monster* really wanted me to die. As such, it mentally prepared me to do whatever it took to do so. Within about a half hour, I started feeling numb. I hadn't eaten anything in over twenty-four hours, and my empty stomach was absolutely not able to hold down all those pills.

So I threw up.

While staring at the floor in the back seat of my Ford Escape, I wondered,

What does this mean?

Will it still work?

Did I puke it all out?

Could there be any left in my system?

Fuck!

What do I do now?

I hope there is still enough in my system.

I was too numb to move, and I was prepared to wait. So I did, for nearly eight hours. At some point, about five to six hours in, I thought,

Am I dying yet?

Is it finally happening?

How much longer?

Is this all I'm going to feel? Or will it hurt more?

How will I know I'm really dying?

Not exactly the type of inner conversation the average person has on a Monday afternoon, yet there I was, having that exact inner conversation.

At some point, I woke up feeling relatively normal and told myself to just call it a day. Clearly, this wasn't working. There was no point in sticking around in the back seat of an SUV in the middle of winter when my life was obviously not going to end at that moment.

Here's the thing: It hadn't really crossed my mind what may have happened outside my car during all that time. It was as if the world had stopped. Anxiety had consumed me, and all that existed was what I could see in front of me.

It never occurred to me that my brother had contacted most of my good friends and family or that police officers were actively searching for a silver 2010 Ford Escape. Or that my aunts had gathered at my parents' house to be by my mother's side while she was losing her mind.

Neither had it occurred to me that ironically enough, if this didn't work, I was going to wind up exactly where I hoped to avoid—the psych ward.

Fuck it.

Not going to die today, so there's no point in sticking around here any longer.

Might as well call Tony and let him know I'm coming home.

As if nothing had happened, I opened my phone to call my brother and find out where he was. As soon as I opened it, my Blackberry started ringing off the hook. The first call I saw coming in was from my cousin Perry. He usually texts me more than he calls, so I was taken aback when I saw his name on my call display. I ignored it, because I only wanted to talk to my brother. As soon as I hit ignore, another call came, and another, and another. Next, text message notifications flooded in. My phone was going berserk.

Finally, I was able to call my brother. Tony answered, and with a frightened voice yelled, "YOU'RE ALIVE! Oh, thank GOD! WHERE ARE YOU?! WHERE ARE YOU? Are you OK? WHERE THE HELL ARE YOU?!"

The gravity of the situation finally began to set in. I did what I could to reassure him I was OK, but I actually couldn't tell him exactly where I was because several hours ago, when I was anxious beyond measure, my brain hadn't really registered what street I had turned onto. I finished telling him I was OK and got out of the car to figure out my location, but my legs didn't want to follow. They felt very heavy, and I almost fell. I had to hold my legs from just above my knee and lift them one by one to walk to the end of the street. What normally would have been a one-minute walk took a lot longer.

While I was on the phone, slowly and dreadfully making my way to the street corner, I heard my brother talking to someone else on another phone and my mom crying very loudly. That's what really drove home the gravity of the situation.

After telling my brother where I was, the walk back to the car wasn't as bad. Just as I entered the car, before I could even close my door, a police cruiser arrived.

The next morning, I found out that this was the same police officer who had rushed over to my parents' store to file a missing person's report for me. Seven hours or so after that, he was just about to go off duty when he heard through dispatch that the Ford Escape they were looking for was on St. Dominique, near Marie-Anne. He took the call and practically flew over to me.

The officer quickly checked to see if I was injured. I told him I was OK because I had thrown up. He grabbed my bottle of Tylenol and reported to the incoming ambulance how much I had taken, as well as his observations of how much had been regurgitated in the back seat.

Before I knew it, the ambulance arrived, and so had Tony and my mother.

While crying hysterically, my mom pushed through everyone and hugged me, yelling in Greek, "Why would you do such a thing? We all love you. Why would you do this? What did we do to you?"

My brother was also crying, but before he could approach me, the paramedic asked that everyone step aside so I could be taken to the emergency room. And then the judgment really began.

As I lay there in the ambulance, the paramedic told me that I shouldn't have done this—that I had made a lot of people suffer today, and that there's always another solution.

Having little energy to say much, tears rolling down my cheeks, I said, "You'll never understand me."

Chapter 2

"Mom, I Have A Problem"

Here's the thing with major depression—if you've had one episode, you automatically become more susceptible to another during periods of great distress.

I was once a first-year university student, with **no** history of depression and suicide in my family whatsoever, just a history of applying way too much pressure on myself to succeed, something that today I call UNNECESSARY SUFFERING. Age eighteen is when I had the first major depressive episode and it lasted six months. It was debilitating enough for me to have to withdraw from my studies midway through my first semester—after having busted my butt to do well on my midterms, with learning disabilities and all.

In late October 2002, not long after having completed midterms for my first semester majoring in political science at McGill University, I experienced an anxiety attack at the library after realizing that my final exams were going to be cumulative. This meant I would be tested on all the material I had already studied for the midterms plus all the material that followed the midterms.

The problem was, due to my learning disabilities, whatever I had managed to memorize up until that point was as good as gone. I knew I wasn't going to be able to learn new material on top of learning the old material all over again. Hence, the feelings of helplessness and hopelessness began.

My experience in high school wasn't the greatest. I had teachers who truly didn't care and some who looked like they had way better things to do with their time. I also had teachers who simply never should have been allowed to teach. And yes, this is one of those times where the word "should" is very much appropriate (more on this later in the book).

By grade 11, I was convinced I wanted to become a lawyer; I honestly didn't know my ass from my elbow about law; I just heard my dad over the years say his daughter was going to be a lawyer, and hence, I went with that. Because of this path I had "chosen," I opted out of being in classes with science stream students. As a result, they put me in classes with the "dumb students," which is how the teachers referred to those of us who couldn't make it to science. When one of us asked our math teacher to clarify something he just taught, he stared at us condescendingly and, in French, said:

"You will be singing in subway stations."

We could cheat on tests and get away with it. Hence, my learning disabilities went unnoticed throughout my entire high school education. It didn't help that my parents were immigrant workaholics who knew nothing about what high school work entailed and how I was getting by. They had no idea that their daughter would have likely never finished high school if not for the cheating she had to do.

Given my experience, I can't stress enough the importance of carefully choosing a school for your child's secondary education. Those years are an important and formative period in a person's life and can significantly affect their future. They may form friendships that last a lifetime and meet mentors who guide their career paths—or they may have the kind of teachers I did who very much contributed to lowering my self-esteem, self-worth, and self-confidence. Please choose wisely.

Before university, I studied for two extremely challenging years at Marianopolis College. It would take me ten hours of study to get through a single chapter of my textbooks. I didn't have much of a life outside of school and didn't do all the fun "transitionary" activities that most students do as they grow from teens to adults. The library became a second home where I felt comfortable.

Meanwhile, my family, for the most part, believed I was either a "nerd" or a very dedicated student doing everything I could to get into McGill, and that spending so much time studying was normal. But there was absolutely nothing normal about spending that much time in the books when I hadn't even reached university level yet.

For those living outside of Quebec, the first year of this college program is the equivalent of grade twelve in the US. The second year is the equivalent of freshman year (first year) in university.

After countless hours spent in the library, I managed to complete the Marianopolis College program in two years, making the Dean's List during three semesters, and got accepted into McGill University. My goal had been to enter the law program, but I was told that it was best to first do a bachelor's degree in a program like political science, to be better prepared to take on a law degree.

I had applied to two other universities in Montreal, Concordia and U of Montreal, but to make Poppa Manarolis proud, I had to choose the more widely known McGill. But the truth is, Poppa M. never had a single clue about what it takes to complete these programs, how McGill is not the only answer, and how, toward the end of my last semester, while trying to complete a project for my marketing class, I'd had a severe and debilitating anxiety attack.

My mom witnessed it, though, as she momentarily came upstairs from their restaurant to check on my grandmother in our living quarters above. I cried and cried and told her that if I failed this project, I would not get into McGill, and if I didn't get into McGill, I wouldn't become a lawyer, and if I didn't become a lawyer, my life was over. Yes—over.

The pressure was real, yet my family had no idea. Even though my mom was witnessing the side effects of this pressure, she didn't know what to do. She tried to calm me and tell me that my life wouldn't be over, but the conversation didn't open my eyes to other possibilities because she had to run back down to the restaurant for the supper rush.

I eventually calmed down, and when of sound mind, I reached out to my teammates to figure out something else for our group project. Finally, we were able to submit it and receive a passing grade. My Marianopolis days were then officially over, and my McGill ones would begin after the summer of 2002 had ended.

When I started university in September, I soon realized that being at McGill was not going to be a cup of tea. Five classes at McGill were most certainly NOT the equivalent of eight classes at Marianopolis College. The McGill program at large was demanding, and boy, could it ever be taxing on someone who never really cared about political science to begin with.

You would think I would've had a clue after coming out of Marianopolis College that since the classes I loved the most were psychology related that I would major in psychology, but no. The path was clear: law was my future, and political science was the most recommended way to get there.

So, there I was, pressuring myself to get through all this uninteresting material, no study strategies, no concept of self-care, no knowledge of what minimal sleep while applying this much pressure could do to my brain, and no idea yet of the nightmare that awaited me.

By the time I had that 2002 panic attack in the library, I had just read the course curriculum for one of my courses and discovered that for my Introduction to International Relations class, the final exam was going to be cumulative. This threw me off tremendously. I had to read that part again, verify with another student in the class that I understood correctly, and then sit with myself and figure out how on earth I was going to pull that off. The mere idea of restudying all the material I had just regurgitated for the midterm, on top of all the material that we had to learn in the six months that followed, made me very uneasy.

I decided to distract myself and instead moved on to study for another class. When I began to read through the course syllabus for *that* class, dread settled into my stomach. I quickly shuffled through all my folders, looking for the other syllabi, and soon realized that ALL my final exams would be cumulative.

Within moments, I began hyperventilating.

My body was very much sent into a state of fight-or-flight. This was certainly the most intense anxiety I had ever experienced, and the feeling wouldn't go away. I began to cry and ran out of the library where I could cry really loud and not disturb others. I sobbed, choked over my own saliva in the process, and eventually threw up in a corner of the campus grounds.

This was definitely a destabilizing and frightening experience, as I had never lost control of my mind and body like that before. I went back to the library, packed up my stuff, and headed to my next class, where I was unable to concentrate. All I could do was obsess over what I had just learned regarding all my finals and what I could do to get out of it.

But there was no getting out of it. I was no longer in high school where cheat sheets would save the day. I was no longer able to get tests in advance. I was no longer able to get help from my brother the way I had before. Cheating at McGill was a serious academic offense that scared the shit out of me. The mere idea of getting caught contributed to my anxiety, because I thought that without going to McGill and becoming a lawyer, my life would be over.

As I continued to focus on variables I could not control, feelings of helplessness arose. This is why I offer tools today to help people shift their focus to what they **CAN** control, because that is a lot more empowering. Alas, I did not know then what I know and teach now.

Additional depressive symptoms crept up, and in no time, it was blatantly obvious that I had a serious problem.

I no longer slept well or enough. I was no longer interested in attending activities I once enjoyed, such as dance practice. I cried in the shower and anywhere, really. I ate less and less and lived in constant fear of what tomorrow would bring. These symptoms persisted well over two weeks, and one day, I broke down while consulting my psychology textbook from Marianopolis College when I confirmed that I was indeed experiencing depression.

My mom happened to be coming upstairs from the restaurant at that point and noticed what was going on. She immediately tried to run to my rescue, but shortly into my sharing what was going on and what I believed would be best for me, the conversation went south.

"What's wrong, Sophie? What happened? Why are you crying?"

"Mom, I have a problem …"

"What do you mean?"

"Mom … I really can't do this anymore."

"Do what?"

"I can't study anymore. I can't go to class anymore."

With her tone slightly more elevated, as if the blood had already rushed to her head, she said, "What do you mean? Today? Or at all?"

"This semester. I can't finish this semester. I have a problem."

At this point, significantly angrier, she yelled at me, "Are you out of your mind? This can't be happening again! Your brother dropped out of university, and now you? You want to do the same to us?"

"Mom, you don't understand. Please let me read what it says here about what's going on with me. I have a problem."

While yanking me by the shoulder, she said, "The only problem you have is that we spoiled you too damn much! You don't care about anything or anyone. You don't even care about yourself. Look at you, you don't care about your appearance, how you dress, how you carry yourself. You don't do any physical activity or anything to lose weight. You don't help out at the store when I need you anymore, you don't do any chores, you don't offer anything to this family really, and now you want to quit school too?"

"Go ahead. QUIT school. But if you think I am just going to let you sit here all day and not lift a finger, you have another thing coming. You don't want to go to school and do something with your life? Then you're going to work day in and day out at the restaurant for the rest of your life. There's no way you're going to do whatever you want with us and take advantage of us. NO WAY!"

"Mom ... please ... I have a problem."

At that point she walked away because the restaurant delivery line was ringing off the hook. We had an extra phone in our home connected to the restaurant for moments where she had to step away when perhaps the wait staff would be too busy to tend to the incoming calls. My parents definitely didn't have a clue about the concept of work-life balance, and frankly, as a result, for most of my life, up until maybe a couple years ago, neither did I.

Mom wrote down the customer's order, rushed back to the store as the delivery lunch rush was soon to begin, and whatever it was she had intended to come upstairs to get at that point no longer mattered because instead, she'd gotten the disappointment of her life.

Looking back, I understand how scared and helpless my mom felt underneath all that anger. Those are uncomfortable emotions that no one likes to feel, and as usual, anger stepped in to mask what was really happening. It's a lot more comfortable to feel angry than it is to feel whatever is usually beneath it. I have years of experience in providing anger management counselling and have developed more empathy for those who struggle with expressing their anger effectively. Lack of proper education on anger and communication is a contributing factor. I hope that one day my course module on anger will be included in high school curricula worldwide.

Bottom line: I understand where my mom's reaction came from and I continue to be grateful today for all her support and strength throughout these four major depressive episodes that occurred over a fifteen-year span. She is a genuine hero if you ask me, and my goal is to help her heal through writing my next book and future books by involving her in the writing process. I believe this will help her achieve the healing she deserves.

Needless to say, I continued to cry, now with more reason than I had before. All I could do was hope that my big brother would be more understanding and open to what I had to say. He was the person I truly felt the safest being myself with as he was more present in my life growing up than either of my workaholic parents.

Eventually, my brother came home, and I shared my experience with him. I was not met with the same reaction but rather with mild confusion and an unknowingness of what to do. I mentioned to him that a teacher's assistant in one of my classes who saw me struggling had suggested I visit the McGill Counselling Centre and speak to an academic advisor about my options. So, my brother helped me with this. We made some calls, and meetings were arranged to see a counsellor and the academic advisor of my faculty.

The next day, I went to the McGill Counselling Centre for an intake session. For those who don't know, put simply, an intake session is an initial appointment for the counsellor to gather basic information about you and your background. You also learn more about the services available and any other referrals they would like to provide for external services that are highly recommended to complement your treatment plan.

Midway through the intake, it became obvious to the counsellor, who was a graduate student in training, that I was likely going to require help above the scope of what was offered at the centre. She also suggested I speak to my academic advisor as soon as possible to determine the best course of action for my studies.

Shortly after my session, I contacted the academic advisor of my faculty, Paul Olioff, who told me he had a spot for me a little later that same day. Luckily, my brother had waited outside my counselling session and was willing to come with me to see the academic advisor, as I evidently had a hard time keeping my shit together and was pretty worried about what my future held at the university.

I've got to give it to Paul—as I write about this now in 2022, I can very much understand why he was recently awarded the 2022 Dean of Students Award for Excellence in Undergraduate Academic Advising. He was nominated by students and colleagues for his helpfulness and empathy, among many other beautiful qualities. I can vouch that he truly deserves this award.

Twenty years ago, when I entered his office, he made me feel like I was the most important person to him at that moment. In his office, I didn't feel like I needed to be silent and I didn't feel misunderstood, and for that, I was grateful, especially since meeting an academic advisor regarding pausing my studies at such a prestigious university could have very much gone the other way. In fact, if Paul hadn't been so empathetic and understanding, if he hadn't shown me that it was OK to withdraw temporarily from my studies for such a serious reason, and that I would be welcomed back as soon as I recovered, I might not be here today.

The suicidal thinking had already begun; I was just too scared to voice it to anybody. Had I continued to push through my semester with such debilitating anxiety, among other major depressive symptoms, I may have jumped on the metro tracks back then as the thought had crossed my mind a couple times on my way home from class. Paul, if ever you read this … THANK YOU.

I followed the steps Paul suggested, such as seeing a doctor, and also writing an official letter to the dean of my faculty requesting withdrawal from the current semester. The best part, and I say this in the most sarcastic way possible, is when I went to visit my Greek family doctor. After I answered honestly his question about whether I had thoughts of suicide, he replied, "Don't do that. Only stupid people commit suicide."

My eyes still continue to roll so far back into my head when I think of that moment. If you're of Greek origin, I know you probably feel me.

The doctor referred me to a psychologist, but my father, known throughout the area as Johnny Buymore after the name of our family business, was having none of it. "There's no way MY daughter is going to a psychologist." Johnny Buymore's daughter could NOT be seen as "crazy," and going to a psychologist would mean just that. What would people think? What would people say? The way my parents saw it, I hadn't been deprived of anything growing up; how dare I make the family look bad? Again, if you're of Greek origin, I know you feel me, and know that I feel you. So, I threw out the referral and never looked back.

I was left with a prescription for medication that I was too scared to take because I had read about nasty side effects and also heard American TV commercials at night enumerating all the side effects, including that taking said medication may lead to thoughts of suicide and suicide itself. Go figure—the very same thing that was supposed to help treat my depression could also make me want to die. Nope, definitely wasn't feeling it, so I tossed that paper in a drawer and carried on with the last of Paul's recommended steps, including writing my letter to the dean.

As I wrote the letter, I cried, yet I experienced relief, too, as the idea of not having to study for those final exams led to an immeasurable pressure being lifted from my body. Still, writing the letter continued to be difficult, and when I asked my brother to review it, tears rolled down *his* face, as he couldn't believe what was happening to his little sister. He also not-so-secretly feared I wouldn't go back to university after dropping this semester, as he did not go back himself. His feelings of guilt were now also being projected onto me. I went from feeling relieved to experiencing the heaviness of guilt, all in a matter of thirty minutes.

But it had to be done. There was no way I was going to pull off a successful semester.

The next couple months were far from pleasant. It was the first time in my life I had ever experienced such mental torment. Guilt is a major symptom of depression, and my self-worth was very much contingent upon doing well in school and making my parents proud.

That meant self-loathing was very quick to follow in the list of uncomfortable feelings I experienced. I had lost thirty pounds by this point, and definitely would have benefited from a new wardrobe, but when you hate your life as much as I did, shopping for clothing is far from appealing. I also felt very guilty about "going nowhere with my life" and not working, so the idea of spending money on myself was out of the question.

Because we were in the middle of the Christmas season, my father insisted on giving me money to go shopping, and so a few days before Christmas, my brother and Mary, his girlfriend at the time and one of my best friends, took me shopping.

If you've ever wondered why buying things makes you happy, when you buy something, you get a little rush of dopamine, giving you a sense of control or happiness. Dopamine is an essential brain chemical that has a role in our ability to experience pleasure or pain.[4] It has been proven time and time again that a dopamine deficiency can cause symptoms associated with depression, as it drains the joy from life and can leave you feeling apathetic and hopeless, as was the case for me.

So when my father handed me money to go shopping, Tony and Mary momentarily hoped that the

---

[4]https://news.umich.edu/pleasure-and-pain-study-shows-brains-q-pleasure-chemicalq-is-involved-in-response-to-pain-too/

Sophie they knew was back, as my mood did shift quite a bit during that trip. I also really enjoyed buying gifts for friends and family, and hence, the quick surge of dopamine deceived Tony and Mary.

On the way home, I was still riding the high of shopping, but shortly after we walked into our house, and I sat on our living room couch, my dopamine levels dropped along with the bags. It's as if the last few hours had never happened. My parents didn't get to experience what Tony and Mary had and had a hard time believing that the trip didn't do the trick. This may have very well been the first time in their lives when throwing money at a problem didn't actually fix it.

Within a couple days, it was Christmas, and though I was dressed in some of the new clothing I had recently purchased and looked rather attractive, physically, cracking a smile was nearly impossible. I found myself leaving the living room where family was gathered and going to the room next door to sit alone at one end of the couch.

My mom, though busy hosting and doing her usual running around aiming to please everyone at the party, managed to come check on me. She sat next to me on the couch, and with sadness in her voice, started asking why I wouldn't come and spend time with my aunts, uncles, and cousins, whom she knew I loved so very much.

I turned to her with a very hopeless look in my eyes and said, "Mom... I have a problem."

And as a tear rolled down her face, "I know," she said.

Chapter 3

"I'm Really Scared, T. I Don't Wanna Die"

On the day after Christmas, I walked up the street to my dad's meat market. When I entered the building, I noticed my parents and brother were in the office having what seemed like a pretty serious discussion. As I approached, I heard my dad telling my brother, "I don't care what you're in the middle of, drop everything and find your sister the best psychologist in the country."

My brother said he wasn't sure where to start but that he would contact a friend who worked at the Royal Victoria Hospital and ask him for help on the matter.

"I don't care what it costs. What the hell is the point of working this damn hard if I can't make my kid better? Don't come back to the store until you have found someone to help Sophie."

Within a day, I had an appointment set up with Dr. Pearl Rothenberg, a psychologist in Westmount. After conducting my intake, Dr. Rothenberg provided me with the local suicide helpline (Suicide Action Montreal) on a little piece of paper to carry with me in my wallet (keep in mind, this was 2002). She also said to not hesitate to call if ever my thoughts worsened in between sessions.

I will spare you the long details of what ensued during those six months of therapy, but I will mention that throughout our time together, Pearl sent me for multiple tests, including blood work to determine how well my thyroid was functioning. She even had me tested for ADHD, as I had insisted from the very beginning that my issues with concentration and memory existed long before my major depressive episode. Turns out, I did in fact have hypothyroidism (underactive thyroid), a disease I am still treated for today. I also had ADHD, along with other learning disabilities, including an auditory processing disorder.

I remember sitting in the neuropsychologist's office a few days after he had conducted the assessment, listening to what he'd found, and I cried as he shared the results. He thought I might be relieved to find out, but at that point, I hated myself more for "officially" having something wrong with me. Oh, the power of labels.

By the summer of 2003, I had fully recovered and was able to resume my studies in the fall term, this time majoring in psychology, and with the proper and much-needed accommodations from the disability resource centre at my university. I completed my BA in psychology, volunteered in the field, and started a master's in counselling psychology in 2008 at the University of Ottawa. All was well with the world and my mental health—or so I thought.

As I mentioned earlier, if you have lived with major depression, you become susceptible to experiencing it again—something I seemed to have skipped over when studying for my psychology-related midterms and not a topic commonly talked about in society at large.

So, six and a half years after recovering from major depression and just before entering the last semester of my master's, it happened again.

How? How could this happen again? I didn't struggle during my master's anywhere near as much as I did studying for my bachelor's degree, so where was all this coming from?

I had just finished 2009, the most incredible year of my life to that point. My YES year—the year I got to complete two internships and during the process felt so fulfilled when counselling people. The year I fell in love again. The year I traveled to New York on numerous occasions, went to Boston and Toronto, and then Dubai for the first time (where I nearly broke my face while flying off an ATV out in the desert). The year I visited Greece *twice*, met new people, made many new friends, some of whom are still in my life today. How could this happen after having lived THAT kind of year?

Turns out, sleep is important.

So is processing your emotions after a few consecutive losses.

And so is NOT obsessing over the idea of being depressed again.

What I mean by all this is, when saying yes to life, you still need to say yes to sleep. Instead, that year I drove almost two hours to Montreal practically every weekend during my time studying and completing my internships in Ottawa. I abolished the possibility of resting after an intense week in my program. Sleep didn't matter much to me. But, in reality, sleep *really* matters. Simply put, better sleep means no burnout! The better you sleep, the more you optimize your performance and productivity during the day. A productive workday makes room for a stress-free evening wind down, but in 2009, I either studied or went out after class. Winding down wasn't an option in my mind.

Poor sleep can also create difficulties regulating emotions that, in turn, often leave one extra vulnerable to depression in the not-so-distant future.[5] This can happen to every single one of you reading this book, not just those who have already experienced depression. In my case, though, having lived through it already, running on fumes and poor sleep was a recipe for disaster, and it continues to be for me today—which is why learning to say NO to things that don't positively contribute to my mental health has been paramount in my still being around to share this with you today.

As for processing my emotions, in 2009 I left myself no room to grieve after 2008 brought losses that included the end of a friendship, a four-year relationship, and losing my grandma and my dear uncle Nick—a person who supported me the most during my first depressive episode.

Between the loss of my uncle and the relationship, I had an extremely hard time during the holidays and jumped at any opportunity to get out of Montreal. That opportunity came at the end of 2008, when my best friend Olga said she wanted to go to Times Square to watch the ball drop.

I had never been apart from my family on New Year's Eve, and one may have argued that now wasn't the time to do so. Thankfully, I was not met with resistance

---

[5]https://www.ncbi.nlm.nih.gov/pmc/articles/PMC7181893/

from my mom, as she could see I had been through a lot and thought getting away might do me some good.

As Olga and I rode the bus to New York, I read up on the story behind the Times Square ball drop. Each year, thousands gather in Midtown to ring in the new year. At 11:59 p.m., the Waterford Crystal and LED ball begins its descent, and all who have gathered unite to count down the final seconds of the present year and celebrate the beginning of a new year full of hope, challenges, changes, and dreams.

This made me even more excited to ring in the new year with Olga. And that we did! It was a surreal experience to be in Times Square, dancing and singing our hearts out from 4:00 p.m. that day, one moment listening to Lionel Richie live and the next, the Jonas Brothers. They played for us every couple hours until the time came for them to repeat their concert on live television for the millions watching all over the world.

In those last couple minutes, I began to cry. During the countdown, I let all the tears flow. I don't think I'd ever felt so hopeful for a more promising new year ahead, and after the ball had officially dropped, it's as if all the weight of 2008 dropped off my shoulders along with it. Talk about instantly feeling *lighter, freer,* and more *alive.*

I decided right then that 2009 was going to be the best year of my life, and I wasn't going to let ANYTHING stop that. The problem, though, was that it was like I'd shut off a switch and blocked all that had happened. That night could have been the beginning of a very healthy healing process, but instead, it was an overnight mindset metamorphosis that didn't allow for me to go through grief as naturally and honestly as possible.

Here's the thing: Grief is what inevitably happens when you lose something or someone important to you. If you suppress grief and all its associated emotions, you'll delay the healing process, see your feelings explode later, and/or live a very inauthentic life. When faced with loss, moving through grief with self-awareness and courage is important. You can also do this with the help of a counsellor.

When I worked under contract with several employee assistance programs, I saw hundreds of clients a year, and at least a third of those who contacted the service did so because they were having a hard time dealing with a loss or several losses over a short period. We typically saw each other for four to six sessions and worked on alleviating the distress they experienced through different stages of grief, though the intent was *not* to speed up its process.

By providing strategies and tools on how to better navigate their feelings of guilt and sadness, how to better cope with their anger, and how to reduce anxiety and improve sleep, I essentially helped my clients reduce, if not eliminate, the unnecessary part of the suffering they experienced. Bottom line, you don't have to process grief on your own, and I highly recommend you don't.

While dealing with grief, often we want to speed through it, get it over with, be done with it—but we need to honor it and give it our time and attention until it gradually loses strength. The thing is, what I know and teach now, and what I knew then, is completely different. That night in Times Square, I had decided that 2009 was going to be the best year of my life, and I wasn't going to let *anything* stop that. Meanwhile, I had recently experienced multiple stunning losses. Being able to make mindset shifts in life is important to move forward and grow, but there's a time and place for everything, and at that point, a very abrupt and intensive mindset shift was not the answer.

By ignoring my grief and need for sleep, I spent 2009 having the time of my life, which meant that no one expected what happened at the end of that marvelous year.

I felt burned out throughout November 2009. I was stressed and fatigued, but I pushed through it all to complete my second internship and second-to-last semester. If left untreated, though, burnout can become part of one's everyday life and eventually lead to anxiety and/or depression. There's truly a fine line between burnout and depression, and if one isn't careful, crossing to the dark side where the *monster* takes over is inevitable.

Burnout symptoms vary depending on which phase of burnout you're in. In general, symptoms may present as physical, emotional, or behavioral.

Physical symptoms include:

- feeling tired
- difficulty sleeping
- a change in appetite
- headaches or muscle pain

Emotional symptoms include:

- lacking motivation
- feelings of self-doubt
- failure or loneliness
- feelings of dissatisfaction

Behavioral symptoms include:

- social isolation
- not performing your responsibilities
- work-related anger outbursts

So here I was, in December 2009, back in Montreal experiencing a lot of the above symptoms. Toward the middle of the month, I no longer wanted to leave my basement and didn't really care to see anyone. I clearly needed a break.

Christmas Day rolled around, and I'm pretty sure I was myself, but by Boxing Day and the days that followed, I was even more fatigued and did not want to do anything other than rot in front of my television. This did not sit well with my mom, and she felt very anxious upon seeing the similarities of what I'd experienced in December 2002 and what I was now experiencing in December 2009.

My mom was concerned more and more as the days went by, and she expressed to Olga her fears of my possibly being depressed again. About four days before New Year's Day of 2010, while watching TV in the basement, Olga suggested we go get coffee with a friend. I said I wasn't in the mood, and Olga said, "Sophs … Do you think you might be depressed?"

Stupefied, I asked, "What? Where the fuck did that come from?"

"Well … you haven't been yourself lately, and your mom is pretty sure that you are going through what you did back in your first year at McGill."

"What?"

"Babe … I don't know, I didn't know you back then, so I'm not sure what she's talking about exactly, but she's too afraid to approach you with this and has been expressing her concerns to me quite a bit lately."

I was in shock. "No," I said, "there's no way I'm depressed again. No fuckin' way!"

I paused for a moment and thought about what Olga had just said … what my mom was thinking … how I had been acting throughout December. Before I knew it, the blood rushed to my head and an anxiety attack was upon me.

"No. This can't be happening … not again … No! I can't go through that again, Olga. No, she's wrong! There's no way!"

"Babe, calm down. I was just asking if you might be depressed, I'm not telling you that you are. Breathe. We can figure this out."

"Olga, you don't understand. I really can't go through that ever again. It was awful, just fuckin' awful!"

"I hear you, but please calm down. We will look for someone who can help us figure this out. I doubt we can find anyone this week, given it's the holidays, but next week we can call a psychologist and see what they think?"

At that very moment, I was officially fucked.

Being next-level anxious, I began to obsess over the idea of being depressed. Focused very much on things I could not control, I started to read online about depression and got very little sleep in the process as my thoughts raced every night after that. Before you knew it, I was very much DEPRESSED. The words *self-fulfilling prophecy* couldn't more accurately describe what had just gone down.

A few days after a very difficult New Year's Eve where I felt so anxious the entire time, I rang in the new year crying in my mother's arms. Unfortunately, it was time to go back to Ottawa to resume my final semester. I had officially made myself sick and had no idea how I would finish a semester as well as the second part of a two-term internship at the Paul Menton Centre (PMC) for Students with Disabilities at Carleton University.

Yet, my family insisted. They told me I had to believe everything would be OK and that it would be. Probably some of the dumbest advice you can give a person suffering from depression, but my first episode hadn't really taught them the right or wrong thing to say when I am depressed, however mild, moderate, or severe the episode.

The anxiety persisted. The sleepless nights piled up, and the episode intensified. I cried every day and begged my family to let me come back home as there was no way I could get through that semester. I told my internship supervisor what was going on, and he suggested I take some time off to recover and regroup before making a final decision on dropping the semester. I then spoke to the professors whose classes I was registered for, and they were also OK with my supervisor's suggestion to take a week or two to assess my situation. By nightfall, I was back in Montreal.

The more time I had to think, and the more time I was not being treated for my anxiety and sleep disturbance, the more things worsened and the more I leaned toward not going back. About a week later, Olga drove my car to Ottawa as I couldn't go very far without an emotional breakdown, and she didn't want me to risk my life or anyone else's. I dreaded going to my supervisor, as I felt like a complete failure and ashamed to not be completing the second part of the internship they had hired me for. I was leaving them in a jam as all the students already had secured their internships by that point, and they wouldn't be able to find anyone else, which contributed to my self-loathing quite a bit.

My supervisor, Boris, had a very hard time wrapping his head around what he heard me tell him as I already started accentuating my disabilities and speaking about being incapable of fulfilling what they needed for the semester. There was a sharp contrast between what he had seen me accomplish and what I was reporting about myself and my capabilities. He appeared saddened by what was going on and proceeded to highlight the great work I had done the previous semester. For a moment, I felt bad, like perhaps I was making a big mistake—but that moment came and went because that's how the *monster* rolls.

That day continued to be very upsetting, as I moved out of my apartment and said goodbye to my roommate Maria, whom I considered like a sister. I felt guilty for leaving her on such short notice that she wouldn't be able to rent out my room. I felt guilty for this happening to me again and for my having to withdraw my studies from this university. I also felt guilty for leaving this one particular student behind at the Paul Menton Centre, a young man with schizophrenia who had connected with me in a way he hadn't with any other therapist.

I felt guilty for all the money my parents had spent on my education that the *monster* had already convinced me I was not even going to complete. I felt guilty for everything I had done throughout 2009 because in my mind, it now appeared as if I truly didn't deserve any of it. I felt guilty for my existence, really ... and guilt is not only a symptom of depression but is majorly correlated with suicidal ideation.[6] The more guilt I felt, the more I hated myself; the more I hated myself, the more I started considering putting an end to my wretched life.

After being home for a week, the anxiety and guilt persisted, and the delusions inevitably began. I started realizing how dependent I had been on family for a lot of things until the age of twenty-six and fixated on this idea

---

[6]https://bpspsychub.onlinelibrary.wiley.com/doi/10.1111/bjc.12291

that if suddenly my parents and my brother all passed away, I wouldn't be able to survive, let alone make it in life. I started believing that because of my disabilities and my familial dependence, I would need to live in a centre of some kind where I would be taken care of, which then led me to google the possibilities.

In no time, I called the Douglas Mental Health Institute and while extremely scared and crying hysterically, I asked if they could keep me—I pleaded with them, really.

My mom, who could hear me crying, came into my room and out of fear, I hung up. What was I afraid of? That she would scold me again if I told her I had a problem? Maybe—because that painful experience from seven years prior had left a mark, and when feeling anxious, traumatic experiences rush to the fore, as do irrational fears.

I was practically choking from fear—fear of my mom not understanding that I needed to be placed, fear of her not wanting to take me to the Douglas, fear of her not getting me the kind of help the *monster* had convinced me I needed.

Quickly dropping to my knees as she approached my desk, I said, "Mom, please take me to the Douglas. Please, please, it's the only place that can take care of me."

"What are you saying take care of you? We are here for you, you don't have to go anywhere else!"

"Yes, but Ma, what if you die tomorrow?"

"Sophie!"

"What if you and Daddy and Tony all die in a car accident?"

"Sophie! Stop!"

"Mom, think about it, please. If you die, I can't live on my own. I can't do anything! Even if you leave me money or this house, I will not be able to manage it. I need someone to take care of me. PLEASE BELIEVE ME!"

"Sophie! I am not taking you to the Douglas. You're not crazy. Stop this nonsense. Wake up, please. Please wake up, this is not you. STOP!"

"Mom, I need help. Please."

"Yes, you do—that is clear to me now, and we will get you help, but you are not going to the Douglas!"

She then helped me stand, hugged me, and asked me to leave my computer and my room assuming that if "out of sight," this new idea would be "out of mind." My computer being out of sight, though, wasn't going to make a difference, because the *monster* had very much taken over my mind.

Later in the day, when my brother came home from work, I begged him to take me to the Douglas Hospital, to lock me up permanently because of how convinced I was that I'd never be able to fend for myself, given I was "intellectually disabled" and all. My anxiety was through the roof that day, and I wasn't equipped with strategies to reduce it.

It wasn't clicking to me that the methods I taught my internship clients to manage their anger would also help me reduce my anxiety. It's like whatever education and experience I had by that point had gone out the window, the anxiety too intense to think or see clearly.

And so, Tony agreed to take me to the Douglas, but while we waited in the emergency unit waiting room, he turned to me and said, "I'm not leaving you here. We're just waiting to see a doctor and make sure he gets it this time. There's NO WAY I'm leaving here without you today."

Though I was comforted knowing my brother was there for me, I still felt pretty anxious at the idea of not being kept there as the *monster* had me convinced *this* was the only way for me to get through life.

We were eventually seen by Dr. Farquhar. I told him my whole story, and that he really needed to keep me there. While he validated my struggle, he couldn't disagree more with the option of admission to the psych ward. Telling me this didn't comfort me at all; it only reinforced the belief that no one understood me.

Yet, Dr. Farquhar understood me more than I knew, because he could tell that the *monster* had me saying all this nonsense about being intellectually disabled, as it was absolutely impossible for an intellectually disabled person—however mild the disability—to have completed a bachelor's degree and 90 percent of her master's degree with straight A's. It was just not possible. With that incongruence alone, he knew I was majorly depressed, and delusions were unfortunately very much part of my current experience, an experience I would wish upon no one.

Dr. Farquhar prescribed medications that could help with my sleep, reduce my anxiety, and assist with my ADHD symptoms. The Ritalin I'd tried in 2003 led to shitty side effects, so I never pursued taking it, and either way, it did nothing to aid with my auditory processing and memory challenges, so I didn't see the benefit in putting up with the side effects. This psychiatrist was not recommending something else and told me he would stick by me until we found the medication best suited for my ADHD. He also said it would be difficult to determine at present time how effective this medication would be, given my depressive symptoms were as yet untreated. I was told to be patient and stay the course.

The *monster*, though, had other plans.

***

Before I knew it, I was signed up for an eight-week outpatient program at the Douglas. On my first day, I wondered how the hell I wound up there. There were individuals with severe mental illness who, in my mind, clearly could have benefited from this program. But me? I wasn't mentally ill, I was "retarded."[7] What could this program possibly offer *me*?

I remember feeling very uncomfortable and unable to warm up to anyone, which is odd since I usually jump into groups and start chatting away. I wanted nothing to do with anyone in the program. It is set up in a manner, though, that provides a lot of very valuable group therapy, something I'd observed during internships when I had co-facilitated various therapy groups.

---

[7] See prologue

Can you imagine knowing you did all that, but your mind consistently works against you and convinces you otherwise? I would like you to pause from reading this book for one minute and actively try to convince yourself that you are incapable of doing one thing you know you're good at. As odd as this sounds, pretend you're in front of a judge, and you need to convince him that you are incapable of doing the one thing that pretty much everyone knows you are capable of doing, as if you were trying to do everything in your power to prove your innocence. Take a moment and do this.

A little off-putting isn't it?

Imagine doing this practically every waking minute of your day for a solid six months. As I write, I think back to how much I experienced this and what a nightmare it was to live like this, especially in my last major depressive episode that went on for thirteen brutal months.

Back to the Douglas, about four days into the program, I already couldn't take it anymore. I went home and wrote my first-ever suicide letter. While attending the program those first few days, I hated it so much, I envisioned driving my red G35 into the St. Lawrence River. While I was at the centre, any time we were allowed to view our phones, I searched how difficult it is to free oneself from a submerged vehicle and how long it takes before one completely drowns. I was convinced this was my best way out, and so when I wrote the suicide note, the intention was to drive into the river the next morning as I didn't want to attend that centre another minute.

Knowing my intention for the next day, I didn't sleep well that night. I was scared shitless of what I had set out to do and woke up a couple times an hour as my body progressively felt like it was on fire. It's important to note that the medication I'd started, well, some of it might have helped me sleep, but the rest would not really kick in until two to three weeks later.

So when I woke up, I burst out crying and called my brother to come home from work. Thank God he worked for the family business. Thank God he had the leeway to drop everything whenever I needed him because I would have otherwise cost him his job if he were employed by anyone else, and that would've added even more guilt to an already overflowing plate.

My brother found me hiding under my bedcovers, bundled in a fetal position. He lifted my covers and asked me what was going on. I pointed at my desk, and he picked up the suicide note. Make no mistake, my asking him to read my letter was not a cry for attention—it was a cry for "I really don't wanna die, so please make sure I don't die today."

I peeked out from under the blankets and saw tears rolling down my brother's face. He felt anxious, which physically manifested itself in his gagging. After finishing reading the letter, he cried and asked, "Why would you do this to us? Why? How could you? Don't you realize Mom and Dad will die if you do this?"

"I'm sorry, T."

"Sorry? Sorry? This isn't one of those times *sorry* is going to cut it, kid."

"I'm really scared, T. I don't wanna die."

"And there's no fuckin' way I'm going to let that happen. Get dressed now. I'm taking you back to the emergency."

Chapter 4

Humanity: 1. The *Monster*: 0

As if my brother's day hadn't already been difficult enough, he sat there with me in the emergency department of the Douglas Hospital for about six hours before we were finally seen by Dr. Farquhar. He continued to be patient with me and my persistence regarding being mentally challenged.

Dr. Farquhar did his best to reassure me that in due time, when I recovered from this depressive episode, I would notice a very big difference in my attention, concentration, and memory as a result of the depressive symptoms subsiding and the prescribed ADHD medication going into full effect.

I, though, continued to believe that I had more than ADHD and learning disabilities. I was so exasperated that I couldn't get anyone else to believe this that I just nodded my agreement so we could get the hell out of there. But since I had been brought in after presenting my brother with a suicide note, it was grounds for me to be admitted for at least twenty-four hours for my own safety.

I tried to remain as composed as possible when the doctor brought this up. He also said that the only way I would be able to go home is if my brother signed that he would take full responsibility for my safety that night. My brother looked at me, then the doctor, and asked if we could take a moment or two to think. We stepped out of Dr. Farquhar's office and went back into that dreadful waiting room, and I said, "Fuck! Are you kidding me? I can't go home?"

"Sophs ... calm down," my brother said.

"No, I can't calm down. I don't want to sleep here tonight, damn it!"

"Well, I guess you should have thought of that before writing a suicide note and putting us through fuckin' hell today. Mom has struggled at the store without me, while freaking out about what you considered doing and what is going to happen next. And I have wasted another fuckin' day, so when I tell you to calm down, calm the fuck down so we can figure this out."

Shaken by what he said, I looked down at the floor as I could no longer look him in the eye. "I'm sorry."

"Already told you sorry wasn't going to cut it. Do I have your word that you're not going to try offing yourself tonight?"

I thought to myself that if I were to do this, it was certainly not going to be tonight and certainly not on his watch.

"I promise, T. I'm too tired to do anything at this point. I promise I won't do anything. I'll even sleep in your room if it makes you feel better. Just don't leave me here."

"You have no idea what kind of position you're putting me in. If you do something on my watch, I will never recover from that, you hear me?"

Feeling so bad at the idea of him blaming himself for my suicide, I continued to swear that I would not do anything that night. It was almost as if I was engaged in an internal negotiation with the *monster* for me to never do anything on my brother's watch.

"I hear you, T. Loud and clear. Again, I'm sorry."

After my brother signed the forms handed to him by Dr. Farquhar, we were finally allowed to leave. On the ride home, I asked Tony if it was possible that I go straight to my room or his, and not have to talk to Mom and Dad about what had happened today. Guilt and shame had started seeping in, but I also couldn't handle being misunderstood any further. I knew there was no way I could get through to my mom about my actions—there was no way I could do anything for her to understand. I honestly had nothing left in me at that point to even bother trying.

Luckily, Tony didn't feel compelled to punish me for my actions and agreed for us to skip out on an encounter with my mom and that he would have a conversation with her to calm her down while I was in his room.

Despite everything I had put him through, my big brother was still very willing to protect his little sister and minimize her suffering.

The next day, Tony did not leave for work in the morning. He drove me directly to the outpatient centre himself. I was not looking forward to my encounter with the psychologist and the staff, as clearly they had been informed of my actions of the prior day. But, truth be told, they welcomed me with open arms and didn't make the situation awkward at all. Clearly, I wasn't the only patient in their eight-week program to have ever tried something like this.

Also something that was clear to me is that a lot of the other patients in the program were seasoned, and there was no fooling *them* or avoiding their questioning regarding my not having shown up the day before. I was truly a mystery to a lot of them. On the one hand, they believed what I told them about being intellectually challenged and that perhaps I didn't belong there. On the other hand, I would confuse the hell out of them when I found myself occasionally finishing the sentences of the group facilitators, which is exactly what happened that day.

While in one of the groups just before lunch, as the facilitator demonstrated a tool often used in cognitive behavioral therapy (CBT), one of the patients expressed having a hard time understanding how to apply what they had just been taught. I noticed that after the facilitator gave it another go, the patient still hadn't really fully understood. I instinctively stepped in and started to demonstrate a certain principle in a different way, using an example that would really drive things home. Needless to say, I had the entire group of patients, including the facilitator and her assistant, stumped—and the funny thing is, it wasn't at all obvious to me why that was the case.

Here I was, practically begging them on a daily basis to believe that I was intellectually disabled rather than depressed, and that I did not belong there—and the only truth they could now see was that I didn't belong there as a patient but as a group therapist.

The facilitator then asked me to explain a certain aspect of CBT even further, and I didn't hesitate to do so because I thoroughly enjoyed this approach for the first three quarters of my master's education. As I did this, the psychologist got all the proof they needed that I was very much depressed and that this idea of being intellectually disabled was a delusion more than anything—a delusion the *monster* had fabricated and thoroughly ingrained in my mind.

They pointed out to me what I had just done, hoping I would realize that I am actually not that challenged, and that in due time, I will be OK and on my way back to completing my master's and helping people improve their mental health … save their lives, even.

For the first time since this all began, I felt hopeful, and for a very short moment, I believed what they said—a very short moment, though, because within seconds, the *monster* had stripped me of that hope and had me convinced I was a fraud.

The truth is, I had not stopped fantasizing about driving my car into the river. A couple days later, I woke up determined to just finally do it. I felt some relief with this decision, and even though I would likely be met with psychological resistance when I headed to my destination, I was still oddly relieved with my decision—or so I thought.

Throughout the day, my subconscious dropped little hints, making comments like, "This won't matter too much, anyway," or "It will all be over soon." Little did I know that one of the other group members was paying very close attention to the shit coming out of my mouth that day.

Just before the day was over, in the last group counselling session, the facilitator asked if there was anything I wanted to share with the group. I was a little taken aback with this sudden hot-seat situation, and quickly said, "No." Then I was asked if I'd had any thoughts of suicide that day. That's when I was really stumped. For a second, I wondered if there was a chip in my head recording my plan. My hesitance to respond seemed to confirm what the facilitator suspected. Meanwhile, she wasn't the only one who picked up on what was happening. One of my group mates did, too, and, out of concern, quickly signaled this to the facilitator.

When the facilitator told me that the other patient expressed this concern and wanted to make sure I didn't hurt myself after I left the program, I could not hold back my tears. What I thought was relief earlier in the day paled in comparison to the relief I experienced at that moment—at least that's what my body demonstrated with this release of tears.

Like I have said before, when depressed, deep down we really don't want to die—we want the pain to end. We want the mental torment to *stop*. The *monster* persuades us that death is the only way that will happen, but it's not! The patient who reported his concerns to the facilitator had already been in the program for seven weeks and had seen for himself that things do get better. He, too, was on the brink of suicide in the past, and he regularly considered it at the beginning of the program as well. He told me that he saw himself in me, and his gut told him that I was in danger.

I'd never had a person who barely knew me display such humanity. I broke down and shared with the entire group what I was planning to do once the day at the centre was over. Some were in shock, others had most certainly heard worse, and the patient in question was relieved, knowing he did the right thing by expressing his concerns. I was scared shitless. I had read enough about what drowning feels like that my chosen method to end my life was definitely anxiety provoking.

The group then made me promise I wouldn't drive my car into the river. And unlike the occasion when I promised my brother I wouldn't attempt to die on his watch but knew that I would do so off his watch, this time, no such thought entered my mind. Humanity: 1. The *monster*: 0.

It's very important to note that from the start of the program until the very end, my best friend Olga (who later became family as a result of my being the religious witness at her wedding and eventually the godmother of her first child), came over after work every single day and just sat on the couch in the basement with me for hours. Five days a week, for at least three months. What could we have to say to each other on a daily basis, and especially given I was that depressed and repeating the same spiel over and over?

NOTHING.

She sat with me in silence—and that was OK. More than OK, it contributed to my staying alive during that episode. She was there, on the couch with me, watching whatever show popped up. Imagine that: skimming through channels for a few hours and hoping to land on the occasional movie. But none of that mattered to her or to me. What mattered is that she didn't force me to speak, she didn't judge me when I actually did speak, and she didn't try to fix me. She was just present.

People underestimate the value of being *present* for a friend or loved one in times of distress, especially during depressive episodes. I have had people disappear on me during my episodes simply because they didn't know what to say—so they chose to say and do nothing. As a result of my episodes, I've recognized who really matters in my life.

But is it fair to say that, though, when I know for a fact that the majority of the planet is sorely uneducated about this topic and the conversation is far from normalized? Years later, I realized it wasn't fair to say that … and if I harbored resentment toward anyone who disappeared during those very difficult times of my life, that's because my *shoulds*[8] were contributing to this. All I could do was share my story and teach people what they could do if this ever happened again or if it happened to anyone else they cared about.

***

This is a good time for me to share ways you can help someone you care about who is suffering from depression, and also what to avoid doing or saying when choosing to offer help. Furthermore, I would like to equip you with the tools to intervene if ever someone presents you with thoughts of suicide or if you suspect they are considering harming themselves.

---

[8]Learn about SHOULDs by accessing my FREE eBook, *I Dare You To Love Yourself* at www.selflovesaveslives.com.

I am not in any way proposing you cross your boundaries and limits and indirectly become a therapist here. However, saying the right thing at the right time—before your loved one then hopefully gets professional help—just might save their life.

Recently, when talking to one of my best friends, she questioned whether she did the right thing during my last depressive episode. I realized during our conversation that sharing valuable strategies gained during fifty hours of training from Suicide Action Montreal (S.A.M.) might help readers intervene over the phone with suicidal individuals. When people call the crisis line because they're concerned about someone they know possibly attempting suicide, we do not train the callers to act as therapists.

As such, I repeat: My goal here is not to train you to become one, neither is it to apply any pressure for you to take on such a role. Rather, it is best to defer to a mental health professional.

With that disclaimer out of the way, the following are tips to help you be a source of support for a friend or relative with depression, including what to avoid in the process.

- **Start a conversation—whether it's in person, over the phone, or even via text message.** I'm all about authenticity and real talk, and I think that's the best way to go, so rather than beat around the bush and delay the inevitable, get straight to the point and express your concern. The sooner you do, the sooner you show the person in question you care and that you're there for them. The sooner you deepen your connection, the sooner you get one to open up. Focus on using "I" statements when expressing your feelings to them. Essentially, take ownership of your feelings, and don't point fingers at them by making statements such as, "You haven't been yourself lately," or "You seem to be avoiding hanging out with us lately," or "You are worrying me lately." "You" statements typically create defensiveness all around, and not just in those who are depressed. Consider beginning a sentence with "I'm worried" or "I'm concerned" or "I have been wondering," instead of with a "you" statement. Chances are, the person will feel cared about and will in turn open up to you.

Keep in mind that the person may want to talk about what they feel, but they might not want advice. Typically, we just want to be heard. Even in my case where my situation was extreme and I insisted no one could ever help me, given my intellectual disability, I still felt good when heard. Can't speak so much for the other person doing the hearing, but if you follow my advice and let go of trying to fix your friend or relative, you will feel significantly less helpless when listening to them.

Engage with your friend by asking questions to get more information instead of assuming you understand what they mean. Show interest using your body language as well. Validating their feelings is helpful in fostering a better connection; don't tell them they don't know what they're talking about or that what they're saying is absurd, because believe me, I heard that all too often, which led me to no longer respond to messages or calls from said friend. Subsequently, this resulted in further isolation and time spent in my head.

Also, I would suggest you have an in-person conversation whenever possible and/or at least a video chat. Although your friend may not like talking the first time you ask, it can help to continue telling them you care. If they end up talking about their depression, please don't minimize or compare their experience to someone else's struggle. Telling them things could be so much worse, or demonstrating what you perceive to be worse situations, generally doesn't help. I can vouch that this was absolutely the biggest turnoff for me and led me to shut the person out completely.

Pro tip: Even someone who is not depressed but merely going through a hard time does NOT want to be told things could be worse, so don't do it. To learn more about unhelpful listening behaviors in general, check out my mini course on communication, available at alive316.com.

- **Continue learning about depression on your own.**
  Reading this book is definitely a great start, and if

you ever know of someone else who has a friend or family member struggling with depression, lend them this book, or better yet, get them to buy it so they can also put it on their coffee table and contribute to normalizing the conversation. There's more to learn beyond this book as people experience depression differently, but familiarity with the general symptoms and terminology definitely facilitates a more in-depth conversation with your friend.

Learning about depression also means your friend or loved one won't have to explain what they're experiencing over and over, which is exhausting. No need to become an expert here, but do not go into that conversation completely oblivious either, because you will likely do more harm than good. Yes, depression often involves sadness or low mood, but it often also involves anger and irritability, excessive fatigue or sleep concerns (exacerbated by feeling anger a lot), difficulties with memory and/or concentration (zoning out is pretty normal here), and physical symptoms, such as headaches, stomach distress, and muscle pain, often brought on by excessive anxiety present during a depressive episode. You can have anxiety without depression, but rarely can an individual have depression without anxiety.

To make things easier, I will propose an acronym that I learned during my postgraduate studies that has served as a useful mnemonic to remember symptoms of depression. Many in my field have found this helpful, as have others I've introduced it to:

SIGECAPS! Pronounced "SIG-E-CAPS." Here is what each letter in SIGECAPS stands for:

- **S**leep disturbance: Finds it difficult to fall asleep and stay asleep during the night. Can also have excessive daytime sleepiness or even sleep too much.
- **I**nterest: Decreased or loss of interest in previously enjoyed activities, as well as a decreased ability to feel pleasure.
- **G**uilt feelings: Excessive amounts of guilt, even with no reason, and feelings of worthlessness. Can cause sufferers to believe they're a burden to loved ones and those around them.
- **E**nergy loss: No longer having energy to do things and feeling fatigued with little to no motivation. Symptoms, such as sadness and emptiness, further exacerbate feelings of fatigue.
- **C**oncentration problems: Attention and memory, as well as information processing and decision-making skills, are impaired.

- **A**ppetite changes: Some individuals with depression manifest increased appetite, while others lose their appetite.
- **P**sychomotor functioning (decreased): There is a slowing down or hampering of one's mental or physical activities. This is typically seen in the form of slow thinking or slow body movements.
- **S**uicidal ideation: Often called suicidal thoughts or ideas, this is a broad term used to describe a range of contemplations, wishes, and preoccupations with death and suicide. Thoughts about harming oneself or taking one's own life are essentially present.

The purpose of SIGECAPS is to help people identify the symptoms of depression in themselves or others. It is important to remember that not everyone experiences all the symptoms on this list. Some people may only experience a few while others may experience many.

- **Get therapist referrals.** As you learn more about depression, you will discover more support and treatments for it. We've reached a point where more people than not believe therapy can help, but it is sometimes intimidating to search for a therapist and make an appointment. If you know of a therapist who can provide referral options, that is always helpful. Worthwhile to mention is that establishing a connection with one's therapist can take a couple sessions.

If ever your friend tells you they didn't like or feel comfortable with their therapist, changing therapists is the more suitable option than dropping the idea of therapy altogether. If you don't know a mental health professional personally, you can always offer to help your friend review potential professionals and encourage them to make that first appointment. If they are already in therapy, encourage them to stick with it whenever they feel like cancelling. After a week or so of overthinking and draining the brain, we forget how productive or useful our previous session was. Encourage your friend to stay the course, as this truly is a case where "slow and steady wins the race."

- **Focus on what you can control.** This helps you feel more empowered, and doing the opposite breeds helplessness. One thing you can control during someone else's depressive episode is offering to help with everyday tasks. As I mentioned above, energy and psychomotor function are impacted when depressed, and as a result, many have a hard time doing day-to-day tasks, such as grocery shopping, laundry, or paying bills. Simple activities that otherwise don't require too much thought suddenly become overwhelming. Flat out ask your friend, "What do you need the most help with today?" If you notice that your friend or relative is behind on household chores, find a way to tackle a specific task together as having your company can make the work seem less challenging.

Another thing in your control is letting your friend or relative know you still care about them even when you're unable to spend time with them on a regular basis. Sending a quick text saying you've been thinking about and care for them as they continue to work through depression can be really helpful. On many occasions, especially in my more recent depressive episode, such texts even saved my life. There were moments when I was about to attempt suicide, or heavily considering it, and a text came in from a friend checking on me and changed everything.

Depressed people might withdraw more to avoid reaching out, so don't feel surprised or take it personally if you're suddenly doing more work to maintain your friendship. Even if they won't express it to you at the moment, continuing to be a positive and supportive presence may make all the difference to them, possibly even save their life as it did for me. If that's not a good enough reason for you to stick around, I'm not sure what is.

Another thing individuals with depression find difficult is keeping plans. I recall cancelling plans quite often, which would only add to my feelings of guilt, thereby making me hate my life even more. When someone cancels plans as often as I did, it can lead to people giving up, as was also the case with me and some folks. People typically stop inviting the depressed person to places and they stop trying to include them, which worsens feelings of depression.

Going back to what you can control in all this, don't take it personally when an invitation gets cancelled or a phone call goes ignored.

Another thing you can control is accepting in advance they're unlikely to accept an invite. Some of my good friends had gotten used to it, and luckily never gave up trying, on the off chance I would say yes, depending on who else would be present and what environment we would be going to. Once you've accepted the above and understand there's nothing personal about all this, continue to extend invitations and let your friend know you understand that they may not be able to keep plans during this difficult time. Let them know there's no pressure to come out, and you'll be happy to see them whenever they feel more up to socializing. That last part makes a world of difference to a person who has become obsessed with dying, like I had.

***

Every time I think I'll pause on giving you tips to better handle a situation involving depression, I find myself wanting to share more insight. Of course, I cannot cover everything here, and reaching out to me for a consultation on how to best deal with your situation is an option, but until then, I want to add this one last thing. Nonjudgmentally, imagine yourself in your friend's position. Consider how you would feel and how you would want friends to respond if you were dealing with depressive symptoms, and trust me when I say that self-disclosure can be extremely effective if you have personally experienced depression. By being vulnerable and admitting your understanding, you will give your friend or family member the gift of relief.

I have seen this firsthand while self-disclosing in my sessions over the years, before I made my story available to the public through social media. I have seen it with the feedback I receive through private messages after live sharing parts of my story, and I certainly saw it when I shared it with a friend who was considering suicide and was experiencing depression at the level that I had.

Just be there *with* the person rather than *for* the person. Even if they push you away, let them know you're in it *with* them.

On a side note, please remember that it's OK to take space for yourself if you feel emotionally drained. You may need to consider talking with a therapist or other supportive individual in your life about how you feel, but I cannot stress enough how much patience is required. Depression usually improves with treatment, but it can take time and entail some trial and error. Even a successful course of treatment does not guarantee complete recovery from depression, and your loved one may occasionally still experience symptoms. They'll undoubtedly experience both good and bad days in this shitty process, so don't assume a good day implies they're "fixed." Please try not to lose patience if it seems like they will never get better after a few consecutive bad days. I know I threw a few people off because of some of the good days I had.

There is no clear time frame for healing from depression, and it won't help either of you if you anticipate that they will feel like themselves again after a few weeks of therapy. Make the best of the good days and actively practice gratitude for the good in each other's lives. I suggest you both do a gratitude practice as it can be very helpful, given the effect that doing so has on reducing stress hormones.[9]

You will unquestionably experience more stress during a time someone you love is experiencing depression, so it's also important to take care of your own needs. If you put all your energy into supporting the person you care about, you'll have very little left for yourself and won't be much help to anyone if you are burning out or feeling angry.

Knowing your limits and setting boundaries is never more important than during a time when the *monster* has presented itself in your inner circle. Setting limits with the person is not only beneficial but crucial. Let the person know, for instance, that you're available to talk once you get home from work, but not before, and if you're worried they'll think they can't get in touch with you, offer to assist them in developing a backup plan in case they do need you

---

[9]https://health.ucdavis.edu/medicalcenter/features/2015-2016/11/20151125_gratitude.html

during your working hours. This may entail locating a hotline they can dial or creating a code word they can text you in an emergency.

Instead of attempting to assist every day, you might offer to drop by every other day or perhaps deliver dinner twice a week. Consider including other friends to create a bigger support network, for both of you, really, because as one of my best friends recently told me, it was very helpful for her to have a game plan with another good friend of mine. She reported that when they came together to see me, it was more helpful as they were able to debrief with each other afterward. If they could not make it together, the other would be there for the absent person via call post visit. Again, remember, my depression was pretty major and intense, so having such game plans in place might not be necessary for you if someone you love is dealing with a milder form, but still it's a great option in case you need it. Please make sure to take care of yourself in this process. I'm equally a proponent of preventing caregivers from burning out and becoming depressed as I am of normalizing the conversation surrounding depression.

When shit gets scary, as in, there are possible thoughts or even talk of suicide, indications that your person may be seriously contemplating suicide include:

- talking about death or dying
- buying a weapon
- engaging in more risky or harmful activities
- giving away belongings or donating priceless items

- pushing people away while saying goodbye with more emotion than usual
- talking about feeling trapped and/or wanting a way out

If you believe your friend or loved one is considering suicide, encourage them to call their therapist while you are with them or ask them if you can make the call on their behalf. If the therapist doesn't answer, encourage your friend to send a text that the therapist can see between sessions. I highly recommend you stay with them if the therapist hasn't answered the call, and encourage them to text or call a crisis line. With a simple Google search, you will be able to find the best-suited organization to call in your area.

Depending on the severity of your friend's thoughts, you might need to take them straight to the hospital emergency room, or at the very least stay with them as long as you can until they stop feeling suicidal. Again, I don't expect you to become an expert just from reading this book, and I honestly don't ask that you become one either, unless the mental health field is the direction you're aiming to go in life.

If you're worried about bringing up the subject of suicide as it might be triggering for them, don't be. Trust your intuition. If something feels off about their recent behavior and you've noticed any of the bullet points mentioned above, discussing it is generally beneficial and often a lifesaver.

In order to determine the severity of the situation, find out if they have given it serious thought. I will outline below how you can do so from the training I received in 2008 when I volunteered at Suicide Action Montreal (S.A.M.). This training was for people not in the mental health field, and I truly wish it would be offered as often as CPR is offered to people who are not in the medical field.

Direct questions about suicide include:

1. "Are you having suicidal thoughts?"
2. "Have you felt like you want to end your life?"

These questions can help someone talk about how they are feeling. If the person answers yes to either of these questions, here is what I suggest you say next:

1. "Have you thought about how you might do this?"
2. "Have you had any intention of acting on these thoughts of killing yourself, as opposed to you having the thoughts but you definitely would not act on them?"
3. "Have you started to work out or have you worked out the details of how to kill yourself? Do you intend to carry out this plan?"
4. "In the past three months, have you done anything, started to do anything, or prepared to do anything to end your life?" (You never know when their actual depressive episode began, so although it may seem like it's fairly recent, looks can often deceive in this

case. I would ask this regardless of when you think their troubles started.)

The answers to these questions will very much paint a greater picture of the intensity of the situation.

If they tell you it crossed their mind once, on the one hand, I want to say there's no need to rush them over to the emergency or to call 911. On the other hand, however, if their depression is major (you'll know by how much they belittle themselves and try to convince you of things that are simply not true), then I would take them to the emergency department.

Things grow more worrisome when a person has a plan of some kind that involves a method, location, and date. If there's a method and location, the really important question next is if they already have what they need for the method in mind, and if they have a date. If they plan on doing so within the next twenty-four hours, then they've likely put serious thought into this for some time, something I can most certainly vouch for once again, and immediate action needs to be taken.

If they refuse to let you take them to the emergency room, call the suicide helpline in your area and let them know what's going on. If the lines are clogged, call 911. Before calling 911, though, if you have it in you to be a little deceiving and are willing to tell them you will take them somewhere else, like for a drive to clear your minds and/or a drive-through for comfort food, and then you take them to the emergency instead (or right after), then do that! I personally think there's nothing wrong with a little deception if it increases your chances of saving someone's life. Will this affect how much they trust you during the rest of the episode? Quite possibly. If you know there are others who can show support and be there for the person after they've left the ER, then I would do it.

If you're truly the only person in their circle being supportive, then I would call the helpline and have them do the rest. Either way, after your friend recovers from depression and their judgment is no longer clouded by this *monster*, they will let go of their anger toward you for "deceiving" them and thank you for going that far to save their life.

In the case where your loved one doesn't have a plan or date, the severity of the situation is often lesser, and this is where you can essentially take some time and accentuate their reasons to live.

Take a look at Figure 1 on the next page—the black square with a little white triangle in the corner. The white triangle symbolizes how much your loved one with suicidal thoughts believes they have a reason to live. The rest of the black square symbolizes how much more they are pulled toward ending their life. When you're talking with your person, help them focus on *their* reasons for living and avoid trying to impose *your* reasons for them to stay alive; this is most certainly not the time to guilt the person, so please be sure to keep your "shoulds" in check!

Figure 1

Listen carefully for what they say is their reason to live, or listen for them to express guilt about someone they recognize would be negatively impacted if they went through with ending their life. Work from this, and maybe along the way, another reason to live will be unearthed. Be a bit of a detective—ask questions pertaining to the people they mention and don't hesitate to take them in the direction of sharing great memories they've had with said person and the possibility of creating more memorable moments in the future.

Your mission before getting off the phone or leaving your loved one's home is to move that line in the triangle just a bit higher, essentially making it so the triangle represents that their desire to live has increased even slightly.

This can very much contribute to them holding on longer because they would be reminded that they do in fact matter. Asking your loved one to promise they won't put any of their thoughts into action also can help save their life. Provided the depression isn't as severe as the episodes I have described thus far, that promise can go a long way.

If you happen to be reading this book while experiencing depression and suicidal thinking, you're truly not as alone as you feel. I understand how suicide might seem like the only method of relief—believe me, I do. Your life most certainly matters to at least one person, though, and I truly hope my story helps you hang on until you have fully recovered.

When you do recover, I look forward to hearing from you and will welcome you to join me on this movement of **H**elping **O**pen **P**eople's **E**yes. Together we can do so much, provided you give your life another chance. Promise me you will give us a chance to meet and talk about how we have both beat this *monster*.

Promise?

Chapter 5

"If You Do This Again, You WILL Kill Him"

At the beginning of this book, I told you about my suicide attempt on March 16, 2011. Now, let me tell you about what led up to this heart wrenching day.

Freshly into 2011, about six weeks after completing my master's degree, I was interviewed for an entry-level counselling position for Lifeworks (then part of Ceridian Canada), a resource program that helps employees manage personal issues at work or at home. I had decided early on into 2011 that I would stay in Ottawa for at least another year until I got whatever paperwork and extra courses completed to be able to practice in the province of Quebec. Also, not going to lie, I actually liked my life in Ottawa, as strange as that may sound to most Montrealers.

The interview went well. It appeared that those couple years of volunteer experience in multiple organizations across Montreal, including S.A.M., had paid off. The interviewers were impressed with the kind of crisis situations I found myself handling, even before having completed my training as a counsellor at a graduate level.

By the end of the interview, they asked me if I foresaw any challenges with this job, and given everything I had already described as being able to handle, nothing came to mind.

They asked if I was prepared to wait a month until the next paid training, and I gave a definite yes. Before I knew it, I had a job with a great company, a decent starting salary that I never would've seen in the province of Quebec, with benefits, not too far from home, in a field I was passionate about. Life was good!

Or so I thought …

As I celebrated with my roommate Maria, I began describing to her what the job entailed, and it dawned on me hard and fast that I had not mentioned in the interview that I have ADHD and learning disabilities, including an auditory processing disorder.

Why would that last part specifically matter so much? Well, I would be required to perform my duties as an intake and crisis counsellor in a cubicle in a room with many others also taking calls at the exact same time—yet I could barely, if at all, block out background noise of any kind when spoken to.

When you spoke to me, if someone else was talking in the room, or there was music playing or some kind of noise, however soft or loud, I could not process the information entering my brain. I got through my bachelor's degree at McGill University with very specific and significant accommodation from the Office for Students with Disabilities, including having someone else take notes for me throughout all my classes and taking my exams in a room with no one else but an invigilator. Taking an exam in an auditorium with a few hundred others was impossible for me. The mere tap of someone's pencil on their desk would sabotage my performance.

When studying at the library for endless hours, I had to move around to different areas because just as I'd adjust to a quiet spot, someone else would sit close, ruining my ability to process the information I read in a chapter the minute they typed on their laptop or produced any kind of noise.

How on earth was I going to work in a sea of cubicles with another twenty to thirty people? How was I going to listen to callers express their distress for eight hours a day, with so many coworkers around me talking at the same time when I couldn't get through a couple minutes of talking with someone when there was a lot going on around me? I had mastered the art of pretending to understand and say a word or two of confirmation/validation over the years to not appear stupid, a coping mechanism a lot of people with learning disabilities develop. But this was not going to be an option while on the job—a very serious job that involved a lot of listening.

A wave of anxiety overcame me. Panic set in, and the negative self-talk began. "Wait a minute … Maria! I didn't tell them about having ADHD and learning disabilities. Shit! They asked me if I foresaw any challenges with this job, and I said, 'No, not really. I have helped people with suicidal thoughts and plans before over the phone, which has very much prepared me for this type of work.' Fuck!"

Maria said, "What's the problem then, Sophs? You've been able to work over the phone before. Why are you panicking?"

"Because at the suicide helpline, there were only two other people maximum working, and we didn't always have calls at the same time. I only had one four-hour shift per week. On the off-chance that two calls came in, I would block one ear with my fingers as much as possible, but that was a draining experience every time, and I can't pull that off for an eight-hour shift with back-to-back calls all week long."

"Sophie, everything's going to be OK. The first month is training, anyway. Just see how it goes, and try to see how they might accommodate you."

"They can't accommodate me, Maria. This isn't university. This is the real fuckin' world. No one has patience for people with learning disabilities and ADHD. I wrote a ten-page paper last semester on the topic and read a lot about all the challenges that arise in the workplace. I'm fucked. I won't be able to do this."

"Please, you need to breathe."

Breathing didn't seem to be an option at that point. I felt like a fraud, and the idea that I misled them in the interview troubled me so much that my cortisol levels were through the roof. All I wanted to do was throw up rather than celebrate getting a new job.

Over the next few days, I was very preoccupied with variables I could not control. Doom and gloom appeared to be lurking on the horizon when they, in fact, were not. One can, unfortunately, create their own depressive episode just by focusing on what they can't control.

Needless to say, this is what happened. I soon began to lose sleep, to have recurring, unhelpful negative thoughts, and to break down crying every time I thought about eventually starting this job as such an impostor.

114

This feeling of *impostor syndrome* can be very difficult to move past. It's an awful feeling and can be extremely isolating. It didn't matter that family and friends were showing support and willing to listen; I felt incredibly alone and incapable not only of doing this job but of living my adult life independently. Before I knew it, those same damn obsessive thoughts from the year before, during my second depressive episode, were back.

Then it occurred to me that whatever I had been so worried about the year before in my depressive episode had not actually been resolved. I was still "mentally challenged." I was still "retarded."[10] I completely overlooked that I had gone back to the University of Ottawa to complete the final semester in my master's, and for that to happen (and to even make it into a master's program), it was impossible for me to be intellectually disabled. Well, it's not that I forgot—it's that the *monster* thoroughly convinced me of the impossible, that I was truly a fraud throughout all my studies.

It was back, with a vengeance, and I found myself operating as if I was at least mildly intellectually challenged.

I convinced myself that I couldn't even shop for new clothing for my upcoming job, that I needed my mom to go shopping and that I couldn't do this without her. Maria offered to shop with me so I could get a new wardrobe—for the job I already believed I would not be alive for. The thoughts of suicide had returned, louder than ever.

---

[10] See prologue

My brother and my mom started to suspect that I was going down that path again but desperately hoped that after I finished the first day of training, perhaps I would find a solution for accommodation and my anxiety would decrease or subside altogether. Talk about wishful thinking. The anxiety was so bad and the obsessiveness about being intellectually disabled so intense, there was no way I could explore options for accommodation. Instead, I explored possible options of death. I read and I read, and I planned and I planned.

Day one of Lifeworks' training was officially upon me. That morning, I felt intense heat throughout my body. I don't even know how I was capable of driving myself there, but I did, and when I walked into the building, one of the people who had interviewed me could tell right off the bat that something was not right. The look on my face and the energy I had in the interview versus what it was now was night and day. And yet, I lied through my teeth and insisted I was excited to get started!

My body was on fire for the entire eight hours I was there, which was overwhelming and scary. I couldn't focus, absolutely no information registering throughout the day, and all I wrote on my notepad during the training was my suicide note. There was no way I was going to endure another day like this. No way.

So, at the end of the shift, I set out to park my car in a remote area not too far from home, and muster the "courage" to ingest an entire bottle of Tylenol.

What I didn't expect were messages and calls coming in from my brother and mother who had driven in from Montreal to come get me from Ottawa. That mother's intuition I spoke about in Chapter 1? Yeah, she had a pretty bad feeling things were a lot worse than the year before, and so she and Tony waited for me at my roommate's home to pack up my stuff so I could move back home with them right there and then.

My plans to live in Ottawa the first few years of my career were officially undone, and that disappointment in itself fueled the *monster* who continued to tell me I should die.

Things only worsened over the next couple weeks in Montreal as I felt tremendous guilt for the fact that I had left Ottawa again on unpleasant terms. I never saw it as "I left because I needed to recover" but instead as "I left because I'm an intellectually disabled fraud who will never make it in life." Fixate and obsess on that kind of belief for two weeks straight, and recovery is the last thing that will happen.

In fact, another way one can exacerbate current depressive symptoms or even *create* a depressive episode is by focusing on variables they cannot control. I talk about this all the time in my course and workshops. Focus long enough on variables you can't control, and you will feel very helpless. The more you obsess, the more anxious and frustrated you feel, the more depleted you'll become. The more fatigued you become, your anxiety and anger will in turn intensify—and then guess what? A vicious cycle has officially begun, and you're well on your way to developing depression.

Things out of our control include the past and future, yet people find themselves caught up in both. Focus instead on what you CAN control, and watch how empowered you will feel!

Going back to my last episode, the obsession and hyper-focus led to an insufferable level of helplessness and hopelessness. To top it all off, an event was coming up that, prior to my depressive episode, I'd very much looked forward to. One of my favorite musicians from the island of Crete was coming to play for our association's annual dance. March 12, 2011, was a date I had plugged into my calendar three months prior and had vowed not to miss. I had booked a ten-seater table for my parents, friends from Montreal, and friends who were going to drive in from out of town.

The days before the event, I made it very clear that I absolutely didn't want to go. However, my mother would not have it. As if guilt wasn't already eating me alive, she added even more and reinforced that I "should" come. She wasn't aiming to make my suffering worse—if anything, she hoped it would lift my spirits to attend this event. And it did, actually, for a total of seven minutes.

I know seven minutes sounds very specific, but that's about the average time my favorite Cretan dance lasts. The entire night, I barely said a word, unintentionally making most of the people at our table feel uncomfortable. Meanwhile, anxiety was tearing up my insides and all I wanted to do was scream. Let's just say I was the "elephant at the table."

But at one point, when my favorite seven-minute Cretan dance, a *maleviziotis,* came on again, I couldn't resist. I ran to the dance floor and joined my friends in the circle. Most were shocked, and a minute or so in, a friend called me to the front of the line to do a solo. For the first time in a long time, I felt ALIVE, and I must have hogged that dance and done a solo that lasted most of the song. People stopped dancing and clapped for me the entire way through. I remember looking up and seeing my mom and brother clapping with more hope in their eyes than ever before. I remember wishing that moment would last forever, because I had already decided that some time very soon, I was going to end my life.

A little less than a half hour later, when I saw my parents getting ready to leave, I made it clear that I wanted to leave with them. I would usually be the last to leave any event and literally walk out of the hall at the same time as the staff and cleaning crew.

As they began to say their goodbyes, I became even more anxious as I wanted to see very specific people for one last time. I wanted to hug them and tell them that I've missed them and that I was glad I got to see them. If one looked deep into my eyes, they could tell I was both sad and petrified. I wouldn't give them the chance to see my eyes long enough, though, or to ask me how I've been or when they will see me again.

Toward the end of my farewells, an old friend that I'd lost touch with noticed something was off and asked me if I was OK. I started crying the moment she did but lied and told her to not worry as it would all soon "be OK."

Four days later, the events I described at the start of Chapter 1 occurred. Which brings us to what happened after I told the paramedic, "You'll never understand me."

***

This was my first time in an ambulance, and I truly hope it was my last. The ride to the Royal Victoria Hospital emergency unit was likely no longer than fifteen minutes on the clock, but it felt like hours. When I finally got to the hospital, I was rolled in on the gurney and transferred to a bed in the hallway of the ER, where I stayed for hours, as there was no way a suicide attempt where the person clearly survived was going to take precedence over a "real" emergency.

I do not have actual evidence for this, and I'm not sure if it was the *monster* or my intuition that convinced me to believe this, but it very much seemed like I was unwelcome. I know a lot has changed these last few years, and there's still a lot of change needed, but twelve years ago, things were still deeply misunderstood.

At some point in the night, a doctor came by to tell me the results of my blood work. Apparently, had I been brought any later to the hospital, I was on my way to serious liver failure. I had a hunch my situation wasn't great, judging by the troubled look on the triage nurse's face when she asked how long ago I had ingested 25,000 mg of Tylenol. In fact, I was immediately rushed into the ER hallway and injected with an antidote of some kind.

So, when that doctor came to see me in the wee hours to report my results, she told me that normal ACT levels in a liver shouldn't be higher than 36 U/L (I will spare you the medical details; a Google search on the topic gave me all I needed to know), and mine had reached 1000 U/L. Imagine if I hadn't thrown up shortly after ingesting all that Tylenol. Actually, don't imagine that. Imagine, though, being told this news by a doctor with a judgmental look on her face. She was basically telling me how close I came to liver failure with an expression that said, "You're a fuckin' idiot."

My brother stayed by my side for a couple hours, and then Olga came by to give me a hug and tell me how much she loved me. She also said an old friend of mine, who I'd recently had a bullshit falling-out with, had come to the hospital with her, but he was waiting outside as he was too scared to come in. Visiting a friend hospitalized for a suicide attempt is uncomfortable because the conversation around all this has yet to be normalized.

A couple hours after the visit from the doctor, my mom appeared. This encounter was very different from the one we had about nine hours earlier when she and Tony showed up at the location of my attempted suicide. This time, she shook me. Yes, she literally grabbed me by the shoulders as I lay in the bed, yelled at me for about thirty seconds (which felt like a lot longer as I was drained as hell and mortified all in one), and then she left.

In a single minute, she managed to show me the magnitude of her shame and anger. In that same minute, not only did I wish I had never turned on my cell phone when I did, I went as far as to wish I had never been born.

About ten hours after that, I was finally taken to a room (or more of a section blocked off by curtains) where I would remain until there was a room available in the psych ward. Again, everything I wanted to avoid by ending my life was going to come my way, and come my way hard.

By evening, two other great friends came to visit at the same time, completely unplanned—Fotini, practically a sister, and my good friend Theo who had assisted my brother the year before in his quest to find me a psychiatrist. There were many awkward silences during their visit; as I said earlier, visiting a friend who has tried to end their life is an uncommon occurrence for most people. And what made it even more awkward was what followed next. My brother walked in … with … my … dad.

There he was, Johnny "Buymore" himself, staring at his pretty, broken daughter lying on a hospital bed the day after she tried to end her life. The man who moved to Canada in his late twenties and worked harder than anyone I know to start his own businesses and continue to work harder than anyone I know (except my mom), to start a family and provide for them, in abundance, even. There he was, looking more powerless than ever, a deep sadness on his face and tears in his eyes. Tears of sorrow as well as

122

relief, as he got to see with his own eyes that his little girl was still alive.

He put his hand on my ankle, looked in my eyes, let some of those tears roll down his face, and in no time disappeared behind the curtain that separated me from everyone else. My brother left to walk my dad to his car, and my two good friends bore witness to it—one of the most heartbreaking moments of my life.

It was, to a certain extent, embarrassing, given the shame I already felt for what I had just put my family through. To top off the guilt and shame, my friend Theo inadvertently added to it when he leaned over me and said, "Did you see the look on his face?"

"Yes …"

"Did you see all that pain?"

"Yes."

"Good. I hope that image of his face stays with you forever so that the next time you decide to do something stupid, you will remember it! Because if you do this again, you WILL kill him."

At that moment, I wished I was already dead.

(Theo, when you read this, I don't aim to make you feel bad. I know how hard nearly losing a friend to suicide could have been, and I know how heartbreaking it was for you to witness what you did. I know that twelve years later, you understand way more than you did back then, and I am beyond grateful that you broke through the discomfort of visiting me in the hospital and being present with me in a moment when most people wouldn't be, a moment where I

123

needed someone I care about to be present. I'm grateful for your ongoing support ever since and grateful that you now help me very much in spreading this movement and normalizing the conversation!)

Moments after that, my brother came through the curtain and joined another awkward silence, so uncomfortable that out of nowhere, he displayed the most random excitement.

"Guess what?" he said.

"What?"

"Yesterday was 3:16 Day," he replied, referencing what many WWE fans consider Steve Austin Day.

At that point, I rolled my eyes and turned onto my side. As if I cared what day it was when I tried to die. As if it mattered. As if us growing up as wrestling fans and practically worshiping Stone Cold Steve Austin, a.k.a. Austin 3:16, was even worth mentioning at a time like this. Tony, though, ever since getting on Facebook in 2007 would post on March 16 (3/16) in honor of Stone Cold Steve Austin. So that morning, he woke up and wrote a status saying, "It's 3:16 today! Those who know … you know."

He did not yet know that 3:16 Day was about to take on a whole new meaning for him.

Chapter 6

The Decarie Expressway

In the days that followed, I thought I was being transferred to the psychiatric unit, but there was still not a spot available. I was instead put in some kind of transition unit with a few others also in need of a psych spot and who had more severe illness than I did. For five days, I could hear them screaming at the top of their lungs from up and down the hall.

I was heavily medicated, dressed in a hospital gown, and looked no more alive than a zombie. A few good friends came to visit and saw me in ways they never thought possible. I vividly recall how numb one of my best friends looked when he sat on the bed across from me and tried to process what the hell had happened. I am grateful to those who managed to pierce through that barrier of discomfort and come visit me: Joe, Telly, Mary, Lenio, Stevy Z … From the bottom of my heart, thank you.

Eventually, I was transferred to the Allan Memorial Institute of Psychiatry on the third floor. My level of self-loathing had reached an even higher level, and it was no secret that I had been counting the days to get back out and try again. Yes, despite all that had happened, and still running the risk of not "succeeding" with my next attempt, the *monster* was feeding my urge to try again.

A few hours later, a nurse came to my room to conduct an intake and asked me, "Do you still have thoughts of suicide?"

And I couldn't help but answer bluntly. "You seriously fuckin' think I got over it already?"

This abrupt response stumped the nurse who then asked me for further clarification, at which point I made clear that I didn't love my life any more than I had the week before. Boy, was I in for a real treat following such an honest intake session.

An hour or so later, after having just spoken to my mom on the phone, a psych ward aide came to escort me from my room to another room with nothing more than a bottle of water and a magazine. Make no mistake—this new room wasn't an upgrade. This was an *isolation* room.

As if I didn't hate my existence enough, being secluded in a room with no window, away from any contact with anyone, really didn't help. My anxiety spiked, and although I hadn't considered harming myself while on the unit and was very much going to wait until I got out before attempting to end my life again, all that abruptly changed. To say I started freaking out is an understatement.

Minutes going by seemed like hours. I couldn't believe that I was being punished for honesty about how I felt regarding my life circumstances. I had never expressed that I had an intention or plan to attempt suicide over the coming days or while on the ward. Had I, that type of response would have merited further vigilance, possibly even as far as isolation if I demonstrated any physically aggressive behavior toward myself or others—but that was far from the case.

The sheets of my bed had been stripped for my own safety, as they are commonly used by suicidal folks in psych wards or prisons to hang themselves. So I sat there on my sheetless bed, unable to get comfortable, worried about how long I would have to live this way, worried about not being able to call my mom or my brother, worried about how they wouldn't know why I am no longer reaching out for them, worried about what else could happen to me at this point. All this worry fueled my anxiety and irrationality more and more.

After an hour or so of what felt like I was truly losing my mind, I fixated on the idea of ending my life in the psych ward, in that room, if possible. And yes, it was possible. Painful, no doubt, but possible. But what could I use to end my life in an isolation room designed for prevention of such an act?

When you've reached that level of desperation and have already read everything available online about methods of ending your life, you find a way. From all the knowledge acquired during my depressive episodes, until this day even, if asked to do so, I can scan any room at any time and point out all the possible ways one can attempt to die, and very likely succeed in doing so. That small royal-blue bottle cap usually available on Naya water bottles in Quebec and other parts of Canada, became a potential object of suicide. My only way to go was to choke myself by swallowing it.

Since I have come this far in describing uncomfortable details from my suicide attempts, I figure this is a safe place to keep going. So yes, I tried to choke myself with this bottle cap, and clearly, I did not succeed. What I did succeed in doing is adding more to my traumatic experiences. Despite vomiting, I kept trying, using the same

129

level of possessed determination I'd used while swallowing every tablet of Tylenol just a week prior.

At some point, I had to stop trying, as an aide came by to drop off a tray of food, with plastic cutlery, not allowing me to go eat in the dining area with the other patients. He noticed I had thrown up and assumed I was severely anxious. Within moments, he had come back to clean it up, and during that time, rather than simply eat my food, I assessed if there was any chance I could choke on something in my plate instead.

I momentarily gave up and allowed myself to eat because the medications I was on had increased my appetite tremendously. I told myself I would just try again later, as it clearly didn't look like I was going anywhere for a while. I then decided to wait until the aide came for my tray, to not risk getting interrupted or found too quickly after having choked, should I then succeed this time.

Time passed slowly, and given how understaffed hospitals and psych wards were back then, by being in the isolation room, I was out of sight, out of mind. Luckily, enough time had elapsed from my entry into isolation to the time I'd been waiting for my tray to be picked up that my mom and brother suspected something was wrong, given I hadn't called.

They began to call, and at first weren't given a straight answer as to why I could not come to the phone. Due to their persistence and determination to hear from me directly, eventually, they were told that I was put in isolation and was not allowed to receive or make phone calls. I later heard that my brother blew his top on the poor soul answering the phone at the front desk.

My mom and brother were in a bit of a pickle at the store that day, as it was a busy Monday and two of their valuable staff members had called in sick. Neither of them was able to leave right away to come see me, which frustrated them and compounded their angst. Eventually, they closed the store and showed up at the hospital.

I remember the petrified look on my mom's face when they let her in the isolation room to see me, and she found me sitting on the floor in the corner, looking pretty demented at that point. After she saw that nothing had happened to me, the aide took her out of the room and brought her to the living area to wait for me to be transferred back from isolation to my former room, which was already no longer available as someone else had been admitted to the ward that day.

At that point, my family and I wondered if I'd been put in isolation for my safety as initially told or out of temporary convenience. My brother then swore that he would do everything he could to get me out; I was in there not by our choice but rather per court order, given I'd attempted suicide the week prior.

Fun fact: The aide who put me in isolation (merely following orders from the nurse who had assessed me as a danger to myself) later became the person I looked forward to speaking to the most over the course of my three-week stay. He was a huge Habs fan (the hockey team in

Montreal), and I knew this because when we had the game on TV in the common living area, he would poke his head in as often as he could to catch a glimpse or ask for a score update.

Bedtime for all was before the game would be over, so since I didn't have access to my phone while on the ward, I would look forward to him telling me about it when he started his new shift the next night. Those little moments of positive connection with him were the tiny pockets of happiness I experienced during that time.

Less than four years later, in January 2015, I began working at a private addiction rehab in Montreal, and guess who was the aide during the day shift?

The psychiatrist on the ward, Dr. Theo Kolivakis, was pleasant to talk to and gave me significantly more time in our meetings than I had ever been given by a psychiatrist. I felt comfortable with him and relatively at peace in his presence. But the minute it was time for me to leave his office, my anxiety would rise.

It was evident to him that I didn't belong on the unit, that I was essentially being kept there for safety, and the treatment and assistance he heard me pleading for (again regarding my "intellectual disability") was not going to be found so long as I was still on the ward.

Eventually, I was given a pass to leave on weekends, the first weekend out having to return by 6:00 p.m., the second one, being allowed to sleep in my own bed on the Saturday night and return by Sunday before bedtime. I had mixed emotions surrounding this pass. On the one hand, I was happy to get the fuck out of there, but on the other, I felt guilt and shame around my family and whoever came by to visit at my parents' home while I was out. I was also quite distressed upon returning to the ward. I thanked Dr. K. for allowing me these passes and would lie through my teeth when telling him I had no thoughts of harming myself while out there.

Every moment I wasn't talking with a family member, I was plotting. Heck, when I was quiet and they were instead doing the talking, even then I was plotting. I am not saying I fooled Dr. K. and that he actually believed everything I said; what I am saying, though, is that I spent a lot of energy trying to deceive him and others so that instead of being returned to isolation, I would be released into society so I could do it again—and get it right this time.

A month or so after my suicide attempt, I was finally released, on the condition I would see a psychologist once a week and return for follow-up with Dr. Kolivakis on a weekly basis, until further notice. And I did just that. I saw the psychologist he recommended. My brother made clear that we were willing to go down the private route, given I would otherwise be put on a long waiting list, and that we would be willing for me to see the psychologist twice a week in the beginning—anything to get me out, and anything to help me recover sooner rather than later.

While I did what Tony promised I would, during the day I would spend a lot of time in my room fantasizing and reading about how I could make it work this time. At night, I would venture out to one of the overpasses of the Decarie Expressway in the very same Ford Escape I tried to end my life in. I parked my car at a different block almost every night, walked to the railing of one of the many overpass options along this highway, and visualized where I would have to jump from to succeed in killing myself. This time, I had to make sure I wouldn't end up back at the Allan.

I kid you not, this happened practically every night for a little over two months. I would walk around near the overpass and look for parts that had less lighting so pedestrians or drivers wouldn't notice me hovering, waiting for the right moment to jump. I wouldn't be gone longer than an hour, to not alarm my family, and would often end my "visualization exercise" with a stop at either the McDonald's or Tim Hortons/Wendy's nearby, and return with a shake or iced cappuccino to minimize their suspicion.

Little did I know, they had installed a tracking device under my car and would have found me in no time if ever I did not answer their call or if I went "missing" for over an hour. Because just as the saying goes, desperate times call for desperate measures.

***

To backtrack a little, before leaving Ottawa, in my despair, I had sought out a psychologist, Dr. Karen Ogston, who worked with children and adults with anxiety, depression, and behavioral and/or developmental difficulties. If it's not obvious by now, I chose her because of her expertise with people with *developmental* difficulties more than anything.

Truth be told, Dr. Ogston really did the best she could to support me during my extreme depressive symptoms and throughout my insistence that my mental and learning challenges were so severe, I would never be able to make it in life. I know how badly I frustrated and discouraged a lot of the mental health professionals I saw nearly every week during most of my depressive episodes, including Karen, but she never gave up on me.

As daunting as I described my future, Dr. Ogston was relentless in helping me see that there's always hope. This is when she recommended that I read a book by a psychiatrist fascinated by how the brain can heal itself. The book was Dr. Norman Doidge's *The Brain That Changes Itself: Stories of Personal Triumph from the Frontiers of Brain Science.*

I couldn't believe she would recommend this book. "But I'm retarded.[11] I won't be able to read and understand this kind of book," I told her.

"If you find it challenging to read, the book is also available in audio format. This should make things easier for you, Sophia. And there's no rush to get through the entire book. Just take your time."

---

[11] See prologue

"I'm slow. I have no choice but to take my time. Either way, this won't change anything. Retardation[11] doesn't go away!"

Or does it? About ninety brutal days following the above conversation, I finally decided to give this book a shot. There I was, lying in bed a couple hours before my usual drive to the Decarie overpass. I was extremely bored, and I thought to myself that I had nothing to lose by listening to the audiobook I'd ordered on Amazon just a week or so prior. Imagine that—it took me a couple months after Dr. Ogston had made the recommendation to purchase the book. Why? Because every day that followed that conversation was a day I thought I was going to manage to end my life—including the days before and after 3:16 Day of 2011.

Even after being hospitalized for four weeks following my suicide attempt, and ESPECIALLY because I had been hospitalized, I truly wanted—or rather, the *monster* had me convinced that I truly wanted—to end my life, STAT.

So I picked up my headphones and gave it a go. As I listened to the table of contents, I realized that Chapter 2 was absolutely the place I wanted to be. The title was "Building Herself a Better Brain—A Woman Labeled 'Retarded' Discovers How to Heal Herself."[12] By this point, it should be apparent why this title pulled me in. My heart actually started racing, and I skipped the introduction and

---

[12] See prologue

Chapter 1 to listen as attentively as possible to what the author was about to tell me in Chapter 2—and boy, am I grateful I did.

The chapter introduces us to Barbara Arrowsmith Young, born in Toronto in the early '50s. She is the woman who built herself a better brain, despite having several areas of cognitive delay. Despite these very distressing challenges, Barbara made significant advancements in brain research that I am very grateful for today, as are many, many others across the globe.

This was the first I had ever heard about this extraordinary woman … the first I was ever exposed to such an exceptional human being who did something so rare in the scientific community! How could this even be?

Well, turns out "her brain was 'asymmetrical,' meaning that these exceptional abilities coexisted with areas of retardation."[13]

Hearing those last few words had me even more attentive than before I started, and I jolted upright. It described in great detail all the difficulties Barbara had experienced because of the areas of "retardation" in her brain. The author's description progressively moved on from major difficulties to *debilitating* difficulties. I was in shock, and oddly enough, grateful that I didn't have things

---

[13] *The Brain That Changes Itself: Stories of Personal Triumph from the Frontiers of Brain Science Paperback.* Dr. Norman Doidge. (December 18, 2007).

anywhere near as bad as the *monster* had me convinced. That thought alone introduced a promising shift.

Imagine this: growing up, Barbara experienced difficulties with real-time understanding and had to review constantly past events to make sense of them. Unfortunately, this led her to face challenges with her relationships and emotional development. This further led to chronic doubt and uncertainty about everything, feeling like she was living in a fog, and like many children with severe learning disabilities, she questioned her own sanity.

I invite you to pause for a moment and try to visualize such an experience for yourself. No, really—pause for a minute or two, and get back to this chapter the moment you've tried to fathom not understanding your life in real time and having to question repeatedly what you've just lived.

I hope you did pause because honestly, most of us take way too many things for granted. I'll bet something like being able to understand what is going on in real-time is one of those things. There are too many events in our day-to-day functioning that we consider a given and, in turn, do not practice gratitude for. If we did, we would realize how much of an abundant life we already have and not walk around with this pervasive feeling of constant wanting, rarely having enough, rarely being enough, and craving more.

If you allow it to, your mind can continuously rob you of opportunities for happiness. FYI—there actually is a better way to live, and if you really want it, I can show you strategies to make gratitude an integral part of your daily experience, so you, too, can continuously reap the benefits of this natural and free stress buster!

Going back to what I was learning while listening to this exceptional audiobook, I found myself connecting with Barbara more and more. Dr. Doidge talked about how one day, during Barbara's graduate studies, a person who ran a clinic for kids with learning disabilities suggested a book by Aleksander Luria. At this clinic, practitioners used treatments based on the accepted theories and understanding of learning disabilities at the time.

This book by Luria spoke of a young Russian lieutenant injured during battle in WWII in May 1943. This man's injuries led to very odd symptoms that Barbara could relate to. When reading parts of this man's diary, she found that his experience very much described her own life. Luria had made sense of this man's problem, and Barbara realized, for the first time, that her cognitive deficit had a specific cause!

All of that sounds pretty amazing, but there was just one crucial problem: Luria's research did not offer a solution. The more aware Barbara became of the extent of her impairment, the more she felt overwhelmed and hopeless. The more she read about all this, the more she thought she could not continue living in this state, and as a result, "on subway platforms she looked for a spot from which to jump for maximum impact."

Needless to say, when hearing that last sentence, I finally felt like someone else out there would understand me. Something I hadn't felt in a very long time, and something that suddenly gave me HOPE.

At age twenty-eight, Barbara came across a paper by Mark Rosenzweig while she was in graduate school. I wish I could spare you the scientific details as I know not everyone is into those, but the details ahead are really key in understanding how this woman did the "impossible." Rosenzweig, from the University of California at Berkeley, studied rats in different environments and found that those in stimulating environments, their brains had more neurotransmitters, were heavier, and had better blood supply than those in nonstimulating environments. He demonstrated neuroplasticity by showing that activity could change the structure of the brain. These findings inspired Barbara, and she saw the brain could be modified, giving her hope that compensation may not be the only solution.

As Dr. Doidge wrote, "[Barbara's] own breakthrough would be to link Rosenzweig's and Luria's research."

At that moment, I stood up. I started to pace in anticipation of what would come next. Did Barbara have the breakthrough she hoped for? The one I was desperately hoping for? What could she have come up with and done for there to be an entire chapter about her in this book?

Essentially, despite struggling with such brain impairments, Barbara isolated and dedicated herself to intense mental exercises in an attempt to overcome her OWN difficulties. Who does that?

Like I said earlier, this was the first time I'd been exposed to such an exceptionally rare human being and scientist, and I hope it isn't the last in my lifetime. Instead of relying on help from others, she focused on exercises that challenged her weakest ability. As she improved, she added more complexities to the exercises. Eventually, Barbara saw improvements not only in her clock-reading skills but also in other areas, such as grammar, math, and logic. She also started to grasp what people were saying as they spoke, and finally, for the first time ever, she could live in real time.

As if that weren't enough, she kept going and going, designing exercises for her other disabilities, such as her challenges with space, limb awareness, and visual impairments, eventually bringing them "up to average level."

And voilà, the power of hope was officially upon me!

In 1980, Barbara and her husband opened the Arrowsmith School in Toronto. After years of further research and development of her exercises, she discovered that individuals with learning difficulties often exhibit milder versions of the cognitive impairments like those seen in Luria's patients. Children and adults applying to the life-altering school undergo extensive assessments lasting up to forty hours to identify their brain's weaknesses and determine if they can be improved. Before the narrator even finished talking about that last part, I grabbed my phone and texted my brother.

"Tony … I am moving to Toronto!"

"What? You don't even want to leave your bedroom, and now suddenly you want to move to Toronto? What the fuck?"

"Tony, I need you to come home. I need you to come listen to this audiobook I just heard to make sure I understood correctly because I don't trust myself. Please … just come."

"What audio is this? Why does this matter so much right now?"

"Because I think I finally found something that can help me. Something that can really change my life. And it sounds too good to be true. But if it is true, I need to move to Toronto."

"I'm on my way."

***

A little before sunset, my brother walked in, grabbed my headphones, and listened.

I nervously watched him, desperately hoping he would hear the same thing I had. A minute or so later, his face lit up, and he snatched the notepad and pen I had in front of me and started writing really fast. He was so focused and so eager to write down everything he heard, it was as if his life depended on it, but it didn't—mine did.

"I'm not crazy, right? You're understanding the same thing I am?"

With hand gestures, he hushed me so he could continue to listen carefully. About five minutes later, before finishing the entire chapter, Tony stood, walked out of my room, and ran down the stairs to make his way to our parents who were sitting on the front porch.

"Sophie's moving to Toronto," he told them.

"What?"

"We found a solution for her, and that solution is in Toronto."

"What do you mean?"

"There's actually a program out there that can help her get rid of all her disabilities!"

My parents were confused, given over and over I had told them there was no "cure for retardation"[14] and that there was no way I would be able to survive on my own. They were also concerned about how this would work, given I would have to live alone in Toronto.

I stood on the sidelines and watched my brother plead with them to give the OK on this because he was desperate to get his little sister help and had never felt this hopeful about anything in his entire life.

To be quite honest, neither had I.

Before I knew it, my brother had googled the Arrowsmith program and was on the phone with someone in charge at the school in Toronto.

Money appeared to not be an object—plus my parents and my brother would likely have sold their souls to the devil if it meant saving my life. So when Tony told my parents that the program was $20,000, there wasn't a single

---

[14] See prologue

objection. Problem was, seconds after, his face changed color because he was told the program was full for September, and I would have to be put on a waiting list for at least a year.

"You don't understand. My sister might not last another year. She attempted suicide a couple months ago and feels so hopeless that I don't think we will be as lucky the next time she tries something like this. There's gotta be a way we can move her up on the list. Something … anything!"

Tony was told that the only other adult program with availability was in Vancouver, unless I was willing to be in a mixed program with mostly children at their sister school in Peterborough, Ontario. Tony replied, "If getting to Vancouver is the only way, then we will find a way. But please confirm as soon as possible if she can join the program in Peterborough."

I looked at my brother and fearfully said, "I wouldn't be able to make it on my own in Vancouver, Tony. I can't make it on my own here because I'm so challenged—how the hell would I make it on the other side of the country?"

"You don't know if Vancouver is where you'll have to go yet, so please relax. But if Vancouver is all we got, then Vancouver it is, and I will move there with you."

Did I really need confirmation that my big brother loved me? Probably not, since he had demonstrated it quite a bit over the years as he helped raise me. But now, with what he was willing to do, he was more than proving it.

The next hour or so, I patiently waited for my brother to receive *the* phone call from the director of the Arrowsmith School in Peterborough to determine if there was space in their school or if he would need to pack up his entire life and move to Vancouver with me.

That was one of the longest hours of my life. Though I had shifted from wanting to plan my next suicide attempt to actually feeling the power of hope come over me, I still couldn't stop the guilt over the idea of my brother dropping everything to move to Vancouver.

The call came in, and my brother answered, putting the director on speaker. He explained my story, and she began to seek clarification …

"Did you say your sister has already completed a master's degree?"

"Yes."

"So she has already gone to university, even reached the master's level *and* completed the master's degree?"

"Yes."

"I must say that in the history of the Arrowsmith School, we have not had an adult sign up for our program after having already made it this far into their studies. I just want to make sure this is what your sister is looking for and that she would be a good fit for this program."

"Believe me, she is. She has struggled with school quite a bit throughout her adult life and keeps repeating to us lately that she would have never been able to graduate if it wasn't for us taking care of everything for her financially.

She never had to work. She chose to do so in the summer, but not for survival purposes."

"I am baffled … I am sorry to hear your sister has had such a difficult experience throughout her education. Her determination is remarkable, and I would really love to meet her."

"Determined, stubborn. Yeah, that's definitely Sophie. How soon can we meet to get this all started?"

"Testing for admission to the program takes place in Toronto, over the course of three to four days. The next week of testing will take place at the end of the month. Would you be able to block off a few days to make it?"

"Just tell me when and where, and we WILL be there."

And there I was…

From beyond hopeless… to beyond hopeful.

For the first time since this all began…

I no longer felt like no one understands me.

I no longer felt this intense level of helplessness.

I no longer felt the urge to jump over the Decarie Expressway.

Chapter 7

"But What Did John 3:16 Really Say?"

September 2011 rolled around, and my mom helped me move to Peterborough, Ontario. We brought my stuff to The Village on Argyle, a private residence with students from all over the world, as well as other young adults who attended the Arrowsmith program. In due time, friendships developed, and some started to feel like family, little brothers and sisters mostly, because at twenty-seven, I was the oldest student living there.

And so here it is. Here is how I began posting at 3:16.

One day, I proudly put on my Habs hockey jersey and sat in the common area on the first floor to catch a Habs versus Leafs game. A couple of my "little brothers" couldn't help but ask why I had "3:16" on my hockey jersey, and I explained that throughout the '90s, I watched wrestling with my big brother. Heck, in 1987, when I was just over three years old, my brother took me to the Montreal Forum to watch WrestleMania III on the big screen with the main event featuring WWF World Heavyweight Champion Hulk Hogan successfully defending his title against André the Giant! (Shout-out to my wrestling fans who know what the hell I'm talking about!)

If you know anything about the WWF (today known as the WWE), in 1996, at the June "King of the Ring" Tournament, the final round match was between Stone Cold Steve Austin and Jake "The Snake" Roberts, now a reverend who'd come out of wrestling retirement to participate in this event. At the end of the match, Austin hit Roberts with his finishing move and went on to win the match and the King of the Ring Tournament.

After the match, Austin mocked Roberts' Bible-preacher gimmick during his coronation as King of the Ring by uttering a quote: *"You sit there and you thump your Bible, and you say your prayers, and it doesn't get you anywhere! Talk about your Psalms, talk about John 3:16 ... Austin 3:16 says I just whipped your ass!"*

That unscripted moment was the birth of Austin 3:16, which turned into a movement on its own among fans in the wrestling world. From 1996 on, I used that number in my passwords, my grad rings, my hockey jerseys, and wherever I could put a number. In fact, my brother and I were so obsessed with the number that one day when fresh concrete had been poured on the sidewalk in front of our driveway, my mom committed an act of vandalism. She took a small tree branch and inscribed our initials and the number *3:16* in the drying concrete. Yes, my mom actually did such a thing—little did I know at that time that this act made my mom a pillar in literally cementing the I'M ALIVE Movement.

After my "little brother" heard my 3:16 story, he then asked, "What did John 3:16 really say?"

I said, "You know what? Good question!" And then I googled it.

This is what the New International Version said: *"For God so loved the world that he gave his one and only Son, that whoever believes in him shall not perish but have eternal life."*

After reading the verse and realizing that I had survived on 3/16 of that year, I was profoundly touched. I felt very much aligned with what the verse said as I immediately associated my survival to my belief in Jesus and that I was protected as such.

I remember the boys looking at me and wondering what had just happened, as there was an obvious shift in me, given the look on my face and the change in my posture. They stared (not so) patiently waiting for me to share what I had just read. And I did.

The Habs game didn't matter anymore. All I could think about was that these two numbers had been such a big part of my life for the fifteen years prior to that moment, and I didn't have a clue about their real meaning. Clearly, I didn't have a clue yet about how much more meaningful they were about to become to a lot of other people in the world.

I texted friends who were aware of what had happened on 3/16/2011, including the verse and what I had just realized. I didn't die that day for a reason, a pretty good one, it seemed, if you judge by the movement that grew out of those two little numbers in the years that followed. The friends and family members I had messaged at that point were all Greek and, for the most part, also unaware of what that verse in the Bible was about because in the Greek Orthodox tradition, Bible verses are not highlighted— instead, entire passages are read and elaborated on during liturgy.

Following their replies and a couple conversations, I resumed watching the hockey game, but this time very much uninterested in the outcome. In the last period, I grabbed the pen on the coffee table and started drawing 3:16 on my left wrist. I honestly don't know what compelled me to do that, but I did, and I started to visualize it as a tattoo.

The next morning, before heading to class, I called Mike's Tattoo Shop in Peterborough and made an appointment for right after school. I got the tattoo. Today, it serves as a reminder of how lucky and grateful I am to be alive.

After that, something else happened out of nowhere. I began sharing a Facebook status every other day, at 3:16 p.m. We didn't have Twitter, Snapchat, or Instagram yet. I would write, "It's 3:16 and I'm having a great coffee" or "It's 3:16 and I'm stuck in traffic" or "It's 3:16 and I'm relishing this killer pizza slice." My brother and I, along with many wrestling fans in the world, used to post on Austin's 3:16 Day, but ever since 3/16/2011, that day had a new meaning for my brother and me.

Before I get into how posting at 3:16 p.m. developed into way more, it's worthwhile to note what came out of my attendance at the Arrowsmith School. I know there will be at least one reader who has struggled with learning disabilities who might benefit from learning about my experience and the possibilities out there!

After undergoing the lengthy but fruitful assessment process, I was told that I would likely need to complete up to two years to fully maximize what the program could offer me. We would need to reassess after the first year to determine if I would benefit from the second year of cognitive training.

Every day, I completed exercises to strengthen targeted areas of weaker brain function that essentially were the cause of my specific learning difficulties. Throughout this book, I have referred to my difficulties as disabilities, as this is the most commonly understood term to describe one's struggles with learning. The Arrowsmith School refers to learning disabilities as *learning difficulties*. The program deals with the root causes of a learning difficulty rather than just managing its symptoms.

Most people think that assistance for students with learning difficulties can only be offered through finding ways to work around their difficulties in the classroom (and inevitably in the workforce later on), whereas the Arrowsmith program seeks to identify each person's area of dysfunction and strengthen it. Ultimately, the program strengthens learning capacities in the areas of reading, writing, mathematics, comprehension, logical reasoning, visual and auditory memory, auditory processing, nonverbal learning, attention, and executive function. Auditory processing, comprehension, attention, and executive function were where I needed the most help.

When June 2012 rolled around, nine months after this program had begun and it was time for reevaluation, I already knew I had come a long way, even without needing to see the assessment results. Beyond the valuable changes I'd already noticed a couple months in, by the end of the program, on one of the last school days, I experienced an emotional moment when I realized I was now able to do something I never had before in my life: I sat in the classroom during recess, a class with elementary school–aged children in the majority, and started reading a book among these very loud children who were holding multiple conversations around me and even occasionally screaming.

I don't even remember how this book wound up there, or if I simply sat at a desk that already had a book on it, but bottom line, curiosity hit, I opened to a page, and I started reading.

Unlike every other time in my life when reading through anything with even the faintest noise was impossible, I suddenly was reading this page, understanding everything it said without having to read a line or a paragraph over and over, while the decibels in the room were pretty high.

I couldn't believe what was happening. I didn't need to reread the page to comprehend, but I found myself rereading it because I couldn't believe what was happening! Midway through my second time reading it, a tear rolled down one cheek, then another. What an incredible moment.

Honest to God, every difficult thing I had gone through in my life up until that point—from my struggles in college and university to my depressive episodes to my suicide attempt and all the accumulated trauma—everything that led to my experiencing that very moment was worth it. EVERYTHING.

Though I didn't believe I needed an assessment to tell me that my brain had changed, I still completed it, and despite having missed probably two months in school days due to trips back to Montreal for my brother's engagement and wedding and other obligations, I had achieved significant gains. It didn't appear that I would need to complete an extra year but was told I might benefit from a part-time year. I told them I would think about it, but then when I realized the part-time program meant I would just need to attend a program a couple of hours a day on Tuesdays and Thursdays to work on one exercise for an entire nine months, I respectfully declined this option.

I didn't much enjoy living in Peterborough, and any chance I got, I drove to Toronto on weekends or even to Montreal at least once a month since that four-and-a-half-hour drive was a piece of cake when it meant I was going back to my family, close friends, and a more vibrant city.

I really wanted to get on with my life and resume helping people. I had spent a good decade and a lot of blood, sweat, and tears working toward this. The time had come to live out my purpose.

On the day of graduation from Arrowsmith, I was pretty emotional and cried when I was called up to receive my certificate along with kids less than half my age. Because of my major depressive episode, I'd been unable to graduate with the friends I'd made while completing my master's degree (I finished it in December 2010 rather than in June 2010 like the rest of them). Then because of my nasty 2011 depressive episode, I missed graduation entirely.

So, here I was, a year or so after the ceremony I had missed, graduating with children from a program that had nothing to do with acquiring any marketable knowledge but rather a strengthened brain to help me thrive in the world ... and change it. The fact that I was part of this ceremony with children who had completed a few years in the Arrowsmith program and were off to live a better life while completing their elementary or high school years made it all the more special. I was so grateful they'd been granted this opportunity to skip the greater suffering in their futures and be at less of a risk of developing the type of mental health issues I'd struggled with for years.

Most of what I do is in the spirit of preventing others from suffering, especially when it's completely self-created and unnecessary. Just knowing these children were going to suffer significantly less than I had to reach my level of education with learning difficulties (and the low self-esteem that came with it) filled me with gratitude. That graduation meant more to me than the master's ceremony I had missed.

I moved back to Montreal shortly after that day and got back into the groove of things over the course of that summer, reconnecting with old friends and making new ones. It definitely felt good to be home, but it was also stressful as I had to readjust to living with my parents while figuring out my next career move. I had studied in Ottawa, and notoriously, Quebec is known for making professionals' lives a living hell when it comes to the equivalency of their studies in the province. As such, getting a job as a counsellor was not possible.

I looked into signing up for a three-year postgraduate program in marital family therapy (MFT), and this seemed like an excellent option, not only so I could be certified and licensed in Quebec but so I could get an MFT certification in the US as well. But—I should have read more into how this program works, specifically their favored approach toward providing couples' counselling, because it was far from aligned with my style of counselling and coaching.

To be honest, I didn't give this psychotherapeutic style of counselling a real shot, as I got a job outside the field as an ambassador for Nespresso and became president of my folklorique dance troupe. My attention was most certainly divided, and I enjoyed leading the dance group to greater endeavors, including planning a four-day dance conference and the group's first-ever performance in Greece. I also got quite a high from the challenge of selling Nespresso machines to the public before they became popular enough for people to buy them without a second thought.

Along the way, my supervisors in the MFT cohort realized this program wasn't for me, and I most certainly realized my energy and personality wasn't for them. One really great thing that came out of that one and only year I completed (minus gained experience from counselling couples and accumulation of additional internship hours that would count toward my Quebec licensure) was meeting an awesome professor by the name of Tom Caplan.

Tom, who taught toward the end of my second semester, was pretty much the only professor I got along with and who liked my personality. Tom was a seasoned marital family therapist, social worker, psychotherapist, professor, supervisor, and author. I hope I didn't miss anything, but overall, he's a badass in the field and among everything mentioned above, he also founded the Montreal Anger Management Centre, for which he still serves as consultant.

In one of my last classes in the program, Tom brought up a needs-related model he had developed that also worked well in the context of anger management. Discouraged with my experience in the program, I sighed and then whispered under my breath, "I miss anger management." I really did not intend for anyone to hear that, nor to interrupt our class (we were a small group of nine), but because I was sitting at a round table relatively close to Tom, he heard me and immediately sought clarification.

"What do you mean, you miss anger management? Were you in an anger management group?"

"No, I co-facilitated a couple during my first internship and then ran my own group by my third internship back at the Elizabeth Fry Society of Ottawa."

"Is this something you would be interested in doing again?"

"Absolutely. I haven't familiarized myself with what's out there in Montreal, as I thought that since I'm not officially a counsellor in this province, I wouldn't be eligible to apply, anyway."

"If you're working toward licensure, then you could work with me as your supervisor. Let's talk after class."

That, right there, was the reason I was meant to join this program, even for just a year.

***

I do want to point out that before running for president of my dance troupe, I had serious hesitation to do so. Having experienced what I had the year before, I lived with constant fear of developing depression again if I put too much on my plate.

I'd been transitioning back to life in Montreal, which was stressful on its own. Additionally, my dad had recently undergone a nine-hour open heart surgery, and I was the one taking him to all follow-ups during his recovery. This coincided with the start of the new MFT program, which was very different from my master's studies.

I recall voicing this at a dance group general assembly, and at the time had been told I need not worry as a separate committee would plan the dance conference and I would simply need to oversee. Planning a trip to Greece was very much not in the cards yet, especially not for an entire dance troupe for only a couple performances. Things did get heavier a lot quicker than anticipated, and combined with losing my job early into 2013 (Nespresso Canada had terminated its contract with the US company that hired me), being put on probation even for the first time in my life in the MFT program, and my dad having a mild stroke while my brother was on vacation in Cuba, I was officially overwhelmed by March.

159

In April, I felt myself burning out and actively chose to take a temporary leave of three to four weeks from the group. That meant not attending dance practices or meetings of any kind nor responding to the high volume of emails.

What I did continue to do—because I still derived some pleasure in the challenge—was to solicit sponsors for our conference, but that's as far as my involvement went for that month.

I also decided to preserve my energy and recuperate by deactivating Facebook. I didn't have Instagram yet, as the app didn't really gain popularity until later that year, but I did spend sufficient time on Facebook, mostly with uploading photos and responding to comments. That took up a lot of my time and energy, so I decided I needed a break. I wasn't sure when I would return, but I truly wanted to learn to live without it.

After I deactivated the account, though, within a few days, an unexpected thing happened. A good friend texted me and asked, "Hey! It's 3:16 ... What are you doing?"

I was surprised to see that it was in fact 3:16 p.m. when that message came in. It occurred to me that because I was no longer on Facebook, people weren't getting my 3:16 p.m. status updates. Something inside me shifted when I received that message, and I wondered how many other people had thought of me at that time.

To my surprise, more messages came in, including emails from those who didn't have my phone number. Imagine that! After receiving those messages and emails at 3:16 p.m., I knew something valuable was going to come out of this, and it would all start by letting people know why I posted at that time, as most of the Facebook contacts I had didn't have the slightest clue of where that came from.

It wasn't time, though … I needed to first regroup, finish what I started with my dance troupe, and complete the first year of my program. I needed to get my shit together, career-wise and figure out what my next steps would be, given I knew deep down there was no way I was going to stick around and complete this graduate program, regardless of the outcome of my probation.

***

In early May 2013, under Tom's supervision, I began seeing clients at the Montreal Anger Management Centre and participated in the facilitation of an anger management group for men before I began one for women. Luckily, there was another female therapist who had joined the team who would be able to take over my group for July as I was scheduled to perform across Northern Greece with my dance group.

That trip was an incredible and exhausting experience that I am very grateful for, but I couldn't wait to get back and resume working toward building my career in Quebec.

Surprisingly enough, months after returning and successfully running my own groups at the centre, I was presented with an opportunity to work as an addictions counsellor in the Dominican Republic at a brand-new private, resort-like rehab facility scheduled to open in late

August 2014. There, I would receive training in addiction counselling from world-renowned addiction intervention, relapse, and recovery specialist Roland Williams.

I was at a point in my life where I wanted to gain more experience in different areas of counselling before determining the specialty where I wanted to settle. My dad's godson had passed away from a terrible overdose at the age of twenty-seven a month prior, which really affected me and sparked my interest in the addictions treatment area. The fact that I had a real itch for an opportunity to become more independent (a theme of concern in all the depressive episodes I had experienced) also contributed to the ease in which I was able to accept this six-month contract that had the potential to grow into something greater.

A couple weeks later, though, my best friend Mike and I came clean about how we felt about each other, and we decided to give us a shot. He knew I had accepted the opportunity and signed this contract and would be leaving in about nine months, yet he still wanted to give us a shot as he strongly believed we would find a way to make it work.

A few days after Mike and I started dating, my dad's body didn't respond well to his blood thinners, and he fainted. We rushed him to the hospital. A couple days after that, when my dad's health was back on track, we cut a cake for my thirtieth birthday in his hospital room. I was leaving my twenties behind and looking forward to better experiences throughout the next decade.

***

When 2014 rolled around, I continued to run groups at the Montreal Anger Management Centre and offer individual counselling under Tom's supervision at the Caplan Therapy Centre as well. I continued to complete the courses required for me to get licensed in Quebec and worked on the website and marketing materials for the rehab centre where I would be working in the Caribbean.

I also deepened my relationship with Mike, which made it harder and harder to anticipate my departure for the Dominican Republic. I believe things played out the way they did for me to live through the unbearable experience of being away from Mike, as I realized how much I wanted to spend the rest of my life with him. The night he drove me to the airport, I was practically hyperventilating from crying.

Three weeks later, I was back in Montreal. Why? Because this opportunity was a bust, and the rehab centre was far from ready to operate. Rather than management informing us of this, I and several other counsellors arrived as initially scheduled, only to waste our time watching people complete the project at an alarmingly slow pace. The only good thing that came out of that three weeks was the training I received from Roland Williams, and I will forever be grateful for that!

When returning to Montreal and informing Roland that I would not be working at the centre in the future, he offered me a huge discount on his Four-Day Relapse Prevention Training scheduled in Santa Monica at the end of the following month. I really enjoyed learning from him and wanted to make this work—and I did! Determination is part of my genetic makeup, and there was no way I was going to miss this.

What an incredible experience! This was my first time in California. The weather was remarkable on October 31, and the training took place at the Grammy Recording Studio in Santa Monica. That last part, on its own, was surreal. That very same night, I went to the annual West Hollywood Halloween Carnival and the following night, I went to a dance featuring Cretan musicians—good friends of mine who happened to be in town at the same time!

The training itself was amazingly practical. I learned so much and developed such great connections as a lot of group work took place throughout. I was given a chance to shine, and unlike what I'd experienced in the MFT program the year before, people were amazed with what I had to offer, and I didn't need to tone down anything about my personality. Only two of us didn't have a history of addiction, but having a master's in counselling and having recovered from depression several times granted me respect from even the skeptics.

During a discussion with the entire group of attendees, one of the participants went as far as to say I triggered her. She repeated it and shared how uncomfortable she felt because of my presence. The way I was able to validate what she felt and recognize her need helped her identify the thought trap that led her to believe what she did and led her to change her mind about me and want to work together throughout the rest of the workshop. Everyone witnessed this, as well as other moments when I didn't hesitate to show vulnerability and use self-disclosure to benefit a potential client (while we practiced). Most were impressed with what I could do and got over the idea of my not having struggled with addiction. "It takes one to know one and to truly help one" suddenly became a thing of the past with a lot of the people there, and I was proud of myself for having been able to achieve that during the four-day workshop.

I returned to Montreal on a mission to put my valuable training into practice and find work in addictions treatment. While I looked for work, I encountered difficulties I never expected. Having a master's degree and the type of training I had overqualified me for the majority of addiction counselling jobs in Quebec. I received rejection after rejection because of this, and one day while discouraged, I found myself distracted and staring at the tattoo on my wrist. I thought to myself, *I have been through much worse in my life—3/16/2011, and my last depressive episode definitely being worse than this.*

Suddenly, I remembered how much my Facebook and Instagram followers associated me with 3:16 p.m. on their clocks or cell phones. I also remembered how inspired a lot of folks felt during the training in Los Angeles upon hearing my story. Quebec rehabs didn't want my help? Quebec made it harder and harder for me to obtain a permit to practice psychotherapy? Well, too bad for Quebec. I was going to find a way to help people one way or the other, and way beyond the borders of Quebec.

What better way to do so than by starting to do something that didn't involve needing a license, permit, or any of my qualifications? What better way than by sharing my story and impacting people's lives by being my authentic self? Why not have people pause at 3:16 p.m. and think of something other than what I'm doing and think of what *they* are grateful to be doing at the moment instead?

Ideas poured through, and when my brother walked into the basement, I shared everything I envisioned doing. I remember him really liking my idea and telling me that whenever I got the ball rolling, he wanted in!

Chapter 8

What Tony Has to Say About the Original 3:16 Day

Shortly after launching the presale of *Depression DOESN'T Discriminate*, I made the first chapter available for free to the public.

I received great feedback that inspired me to keep writing and to keep going with my mission.

Even though I had intended to interview my brother regarding his experience, it was refreshing to see how many people wanted to know more about his experience on 3:16 Day. Some wanted to hear more from my mom as well, but I knew that would have to come at a later date, as there is still a lot of healing that needs to take place before we can interview my mom.

I knew my brother would be up for the task as he always told me he was ready to go all in when the time came to take the I'M ALIVE Movement further, so I didn't hesitate to organize an interview with him.

Sophia: Thank you, big brother, for being here with me today and allowing me to interview you. I know a lot of people would benefit from hearing about your experience as someone dealing with and caregiving for a loved one with depression. I'm going to ask you a couple questions about your experience on March 16, 2011, and the days that followed. I'll start by asking if there's anything you'd like to add or elaborate on from what I've already shared in the free version of Chapter 1.

Tony: Let's go back to the day itself, starting from that morning. I was expecting you at noon at the store.

169

Sophia: I remember.

Tony: On that day, you hadn't shown up by 12:15, and I hadn't noticed that you weren't there yet. Mom remarked and started calling you. You weren't answering. Then by 12:45, she said she had been trying to reach you. Then I tried, and you still were not answering. I kept trying you every ten to fifteen minutes between dealing with clients, and at that point, I was getting progressively more worried.

By two o'clock, I called the police to file a missing person's report. When the police came, I tried to explain what we thought was going on. Then I started searching through my emails, looking for the distressed emails you'd sent me prior to that day. I showed the police officer one of your more recent emails as evidence that you're really in distress. After they read that email, they took things more seriously. They filed the report and left.

At that point, I'm scrambling, trying to figure out where you could be and this time I started calling around to some of our friends, Don Stefano being one of them. Right away, he showed up to the house and we started splitting territory. We then went for a drive together, trying to think of where we could look, at one point so aimlessly driving, we wound up on the mountain.

We came back down the mountain and tried to think. We then each went home and continued to think of potential places you could be. After I mentioned a potential spot, he'd say, "Done," and get back in his car to look for you around that area.

At this point, word had gotten out through Mom, so our cousins started calling me, and other people were calling me back who I'd made a few calls or sent texts to. Actually, I remember when I was in the car with Don Stefano, we called New York. We called Eleni to see if maybe you had reached out to her and if you were basically in your car and on your way there, but she had not heard from you whatsoever. She swore she hadn't heard from you, or else she would have told me. I was like, "Please don't keep it from me. I just need to know that she's safe." And she's like, "No, I really haven't heard anything." She asked me to please text her back if I had any news later.

Later, though, everybody was texting back, everybody at that point, like a massive citywide search party had begun. That evening, while we were driving around searching, back at the house our relatives had gathered. It was a very morbid scene. They were crying in panic. It felt like coming home to a gathering relatives have when they just found out someone has died. Watching them all cry really felt like the precursor to your funeral. Mom was crying so much … it's as if you were gone already. During all that, there was Dad sitting in a corner, not a word coming out of him …

Sophia: How did that feel? Seeing that?

Tony: Fucking horrible. I just wanted to yell at everybody to calm the fuck down. I told them a little more gently, but when you see all these people on a downer or whatever, it brings you down. It was a really morbid feeling walking into the house as if it was too late to save you. You were already gone.

We didn't walk into a search party … we walked into a postmortem. And I really didn't have time to deal with all of them because I was still on the phone calling everywhere I could imagine.

I don't remember what time this was exactly—it was still evening—I stepped outside to get on the phone with Sandra and all of a sudden, the other line started beeping and it was you! And I just yelled out, "OH MY GOD, it's her." I didn't even say bye to Sandra. I just hung up and answered your call. I was like, "Where are you? Where are you?" And it's as if mother heard me or was standing in the vestibule or something—bottom line, she heard me and there was commotion as I ran back in to grab my keys. At this point, I was signaling that it was you on the phone and I needed to run to the car. You were trying to explain to me where you were, but you were groggy and wobbly in what you were saying.

172

I was too busy holding the phone. Holding the keys, trying to start the car … I was scared of dropping the phone or something before finding out where you were. Mother followed me and had nothing but her phone when she got in the car. I think she was even wearing house slippers out in the snow. It's like she saw that I was in such a rush and not going to wait for anybody, she just ran and got in the passenger seat. I didn't want her to get in the car with me, but she got in and I started driving, now that I had you on the phone and you were trying to explain to me where you were. She was freaking panicking. I even yelled at her at one point, "Stop panicking! Fuck, this isn't helping! Do you have your phone with you?" She did, so I told her to call 911.

So she did. I remember I had an iPhone, but she still had one of those old-fashioned phones and she couldn't get it on speaker. I had you on speaker so that I could keep driving. Then I passed my phone to Mom and put hers to my ear to talk to the 911 operator. I was telling the operator what you were telling me and where you were more or less until you finally wobbled to the street corner to tell me that you were on the corner of St. Dominique and Marie-Anne. I repeated that to the operator, and by the time we got there, the cops were already there—and who were they? The ones who came earlier in the day to take our report. One of them grabbed my arm and told me you were OK, but I had to see with my own eyes.

I remember getting past him and poking my head in the car to check on you. I was so relieved to see you were alive. Mother was freaking out and crying, and I saw her push through and talk to you, but it wasn't until reading your first chapter that I knew what exactly she said to you. I just remembered her freaking out while we waited for the ambulance while her practically bare feet were in the snow.

Sophia: Wow … I'll be honest … hearing these extra details is informative yet it makes my stomach uneasy as I have been reliving that day more and more since writing the chapter. I take it this isn't easy for you to recount either.

Tony: No, it's not. But I am willing to keep going if you're up for it.

Sophia: I am.

Tony: Great, let's do this. It did not take too long for the ambulance to arrive, and for some reason … it honestly escapes me right now … they wouldn't let us in the ambulance with you. They said they were going to take you to the Royal Vic, so we drove there and even got there slightly before them. Olga got there shortly after we arrived, as she was the first person I texted after seeing for myself that you were OK.

I remember telling Mom to take my car and go home, which she fought with me at first, but eventually realized there was nothing she could do in the waiting room and that it was best if she went to Dad. So she left, and I stayed and waited until they would let me see you again.

It was a hectic evening. They had you in some hallway in the emergency section, and when I saw there were a couple of rowdy drunks and drug addicts also waiting to be seen in that hallway, there was no way I was leaving you alone. I spent the night with you until 5:00 a.m. when Mom showed up. That was the first time I had to leave your side as two people weren't allowed in at once. I didn't sleep a wink that night because if anybody needed sleep, you needed it more than anything. I was hypervigilant at that point, aiming to protect you from any of the sketchy people I noticed walking near or toward you.

Sophia: I had forgotten about that. I also didn't know about that pre-funeral scene that took place at our home. Ever since you described that scene, my stomach has been upside down.

I have so many other questions regarding details of that day, but the purpose of this interview isn't so much to get caught up in those kinds of details as it is to get a sense of what that all felt like for you.

Ultimately, there are two purposes for this book. One is to normalize the conversation regarding depression, so that people now and in the future do not suffer in silence and openly speak of whatever distress they may be

experiencing that's affecting their mental health. The second purpose is to help open people's eyes to what this *monster* ultimately does to the family, friends, and caregivers of those suffering with depression.

Someone could be reading this book right now who is also experiencing depression, not necessarily at the level described throughout this book but enough to have had thoughts of suicide. If you're that someone who has been told by this *monster* that your family and friends would be better off without you, I want you to know that ultimately, *this* is what a family really goes through when you listen to the *monster*.

If you've been convinced that the family will be better off without you, know that exactly the opposite will happen. The *monster* has a funny way of making you think this will be a walk in the park for them, but the *monster* is lying. I promise.

Someone else could be reading this book who's never experienced depression and who is not actively taking steps to improve or protect their mental health, who is letting stress overtake their lives. A person who is burning out and still not considering taking care of themselves, a person who may not love themselves enough to actually take preventive steps to keep their mental health intact, but who at least loves their significant others and their family members enough to do so. I am hoping that by interviewing you, Tony, and you giving us a real sense of what this was like for you, the person who wouldn't normally invest in their mental health will see that this is what they may eventually put their brother or mom or girlfriend or wife through. If you're that person reading this right now, consider taking better care of your mental health and working toward reducing your stress, or letting go of anger and resentment you've bottled up for some time, or even working on methods to improve your sleep habits. If you aren't willing to do this for yourself, do this for the people who you love and who love you back because what Tony has been describing is what they might go through.

Bringing it back to you, Tony, I know that sharing about all this years later can't be easy … and again, I am very grateful for you wanting to contribute to furthering people's understanding about what it's really like. Would you recommend to someone that they take better care of themselves so that they don't put their family through this shit?

Tony: Obviously, I can't stress that enough … Because truth be told, in certain respects, I was lucky … and so were you.

Sophia: What do you mean?

Tony: Well, through your various episodes, especially this specific one we've been talking about, I took three months off work because I was home taking care of you, pretty much making sure you wouldn't harm yourself. You essentially had to be on a sort of suicide watch after coming out of the psych ward.

We were privileged that I could take off work because we owned our own business and at the time, Mom and Dad weren't as old and still in a position to take care of things without me.

But it was draining. I'd much rather have been at work. It was frustrating. It would make me angry because I couldn't get through to you. You know, going back to the actual day itself, coming home and finding everybody in that morbid state, already crying as if a funeral was coming, that sucks the life out of a person. That day sucked the life out of me.

So had some of the days before then and after because of the damage you did to our parents and how you sucked the life out of them too. It was heartbreaking and draining to watch them constantly sit and cry—even "almighty" Dad, the man who never showed emotions.

It would start off with Mom being a total wreck, which would then bring down Dad, of course. They did whatever they needed to do at work, and then they were just in the office, sitting on their desk chairs, both of them pretty helpless and hopeless. And this went on for months. It started from the time we brought you back from Ottawa to months after your hospitalization and until you discovered the Arrowsmith program.

I had no time to sit there and be depressed and sad for you. Everybody else was sad all around me. I had no time to deal with anything I was feeling. I had to take care of business. I had to take care of you. I didn't have the luxury to feel sad. I would feel anger as I watched THEM be sad. It was angering me that they just couldn't snap out of it and be strong along with me.

Then more anger would come. I'd have anger toward you because you put them in this state, even though you didn't really want to. I'd have anger toward you because I would try to talk to you, and it didn't matter what we told you, you would have a counterargument or you wouldn't care. It didn't matter how logical or how much what I told you made sense, you would not listen. You just didn't care … And that would obviously be frustrating. I went through a lot of anger and frustration more than anything, which was mentally exhausting.

But I never stopped wanting to help you, because you're my sister, and I love you.

Sophia: Can I interrupt you for one second? I am not going to lie, some of my unhealed trauma is coming to the fore, and I find myself feeling guilty, which I know consciously serves no purpose, but at a subconscious level, other things continue to happen. My neck has been tensing up like you can't believe, and I need and want to clarify something.

Now that you've read my first chapter, and you've heard me mention before and as I do throughout this book that depression is a *monster*—now that you've read me saying how much this *monster* was fueling my desire to end my life and that this *monster* was trying to convince me that you guys would be better off without me, that it pervaded my thoughts and led me to zero in on specific things I never would have in a right state of mind—from your experience, as an outsider knowing me and how I am, knowing what a caring individual I usually am and then hearing me say "I don't care," you know I could completely understand how frustrating that was, right? How draining that was for you? How much my behavior would suck the life out of you? I don't doubt that's exactly what was going on at that time. But again, knowing what you knew about me and then seeing me speak in the way I did, and behave the way I did, did it ever give you the impression that someone else had taken over?

Tony: Oh, yeah. I knew where you were going with this before you even finished your last sentence. You had pulled a complete 180. From alive, bubbly, loud, the life of the party, with a glow in your eyes and a smile that would light up any room and a contagious laugh that could wake the dead. We were suddenly exposed to the complete opposite of your good qualities and traits.

It wasn't just the experience of talking to you and you not caring or listening that was draining. Practically everything that would come out of your mouth had us like, "What the fuck? Where's this coming from?"

That just added to my frustration and exhaustion. I was so discouraged and depleted. I could no longer enjoy any hobbies because how could I enjoy anything, knowing what my sister was going through? How could I attend parties or events I was invited to—how could I?

You could say I was probably experiencing symptoms of depression at that point because of how helpless I felt.

Sophia: I saw that you were burning out. That's definitely safe to say. Burnout symptoms are similar to mild depressive symptoms, and very often I tell people to take care of themselves when they feel like they're burning out to prevent depression because there's a fine line between the two, and when you cross over to the other side, it's a lot more life-threatening and a lot harder to recover from.

Whatever the case may be, you were definitely burning out, and with all the descriptors you've given about how energy-sucking the experience was and how fatigued you were … it's safe to say that you were experiencing caregiver burnout. That's a real thing. So is caregiver depression. Maybe you never made it to caregiver depression because you weren't allowing yourself even to

experience certain feelings, for my survival, really, because if you didn't do what you were doing for me, then I don't know if I would have survived. Not because our parents didn't care for me but because of language barriers and whatnot. They couldn't have understood all that you did in the appointments you took me to and with all those professionals you've spoken to throughout these past twenty years since my first depressive episode.

Tony: Yeah … and we could probably talk about this for a very long time, regarding all your episodes, but right now I am really trying to convey the message that depression affects every family member.

You know, Mom can't give you an interview right now, but I can tell you at least a little of the effect that your 2011 depression had on her. It was truly heartbreaking to see Mom during that time. At that point, she no longer cared for anything or anyone but you, obviously. If something happened to you, it would have been the end of her life as well. I think she would have committed suicide following you and not even thought about me or Dad. That's the effect it had on her. She lost her wits. She was no longer the person we knew. She was constantly crying. This *monster* sucked the life out of her.

I can't find the words to do any of this justice for people to truly understand how important it is to not let their mental health get to that point.

Sophia: Thank you for this, Tony. I know it's hard to find the words, especially when we are aiming to get this message out to people who've never experienced depression.

Like the book title says, *Depression DOESN'T Discriminate*, I really hope to get through to the person who thinks they're immune to depression, and who is just carrying on burning out or adding even more pressure to themselves. Especially to those living in the pressure cooker known as North America.

This message is really for the person not taking steps to check in with themselves, not taking steps to listen to their needs, not taking steps to love themselves, not taking steps to let go of anger. If you're one of those people and you're not willing to take preventive measures for yourself, then do it for the ones you love because, holy shit, do they ever go through a debilitating experience themselves!

Once you're depressed, you don't care much. It's like my capacity to feel love was lost. I can't explain it, but I love you guys so damn much, and I couldn't feel love for anyone or anything at that point.

Tony: I recall. It didn't matter what we were going through. You didn't care, and you were so convinced that ending your life would put an end to your suffering and that we would no longer feel burdened.

183

Depression DOESN'T Discriminate

When you were depressed, it didn't matter to you what we were going through. Or if it ever did, it was for a very short moment. You didn't care what damage was done to any relative. It's as if you were forbidden to care.

I wish I had the words. As educated as I am, I can't find the words to help someone really understand. I wish I had the words that would make them understand what I couldn't even make you understand then.

Please, if you're burning out, think twice before you push further through your burnout. Once you get deeper into it and become depressed, there's practically no turning back if you don't have a good support network and the right treatment.

You had me by your side, but unfortunately, others don't. I didn't have a wife and daughter at the time of that episode. Other people may also have a close sibling, but if that sibling is married with their own kids, they won't have as much time to spend as I did with you. Definitely not because they don't care, but because their lives are much more demanding.

Sophia: Everything you're saying about not having the words makes sense. A healer once told me that depression belongs to another dimension, and that is why in this dimension, we don't have the words to properly describe what this experience is like.

That resonated with me. Just the idea that it's from another dimension, and that's why we cannot find the words in this dimension to express what it's really like, brought some peace at that point.

Even though I have lived with major depression four times, I still can't find the words to give you an accurate representation of this *monster*, as it belongs to another dimension.

Tony: I hope my words have been enough to describe my experience as a caregiver … to at least help the family members of those who are going through it know that they are not alone, and that there is support for them out there. If ever they seek me out online or in person and want to talk more about this, I'm there for absolutely anybody.

Sophia: Thanks, T. I am grateful for how much you want to contribute to this movement and help people.

Earlier when I asked you if you felt at any point that someone or something else had taken over my mind, you said, "Yeah, obviously." I hope that brings solace to caregivers and others who have loved ones experiencing depression because then hopefully, they'll realize that this isn't personal. Ultimately, the person suffering with depression isn't doing this on purpose and isn't actively trying to hurt their feelings and drain the hell out of them. It is like something else has taken over!

Tony: Yes. I can indeed attest to that. It was not you. You were taken over. Whether it was something from another dimension, or whatever you want to call it, that was not you. That was not anything like you. Some of the anger and hate that came out of you in that state … wow, was that ever nothing like you. It's like you were not my sister anymore, even though you were.

***

Whether you've bought this book because you want to support me, or you're someone who has known someone who's taken their life and can't quite wrap your head around it, or you've had a colleague who had to leave work due to depression and has kind of left you in a pickle in the meantime—whoever you may be, without trying to scare you, I want you to know that it can happen to you too.

I hope this opens your eyes to realize that if you don't take active steps to improve your mental health—or as I often call it, emotional wealth—then it can happen to you too.

People are driven to acquire financial wealth, but they do not realize that without emotional wealth, financial wealth is pointless. I want people to realize that without emotional wealth, without taking steps toward acquiring emotional wealth and protecting their mental health, they could end up fucking shit up for everyone else in their life.

Because that's really what happened here—I fucked shit up for the people I love. If you don't want to fuck shit up for the people you love, remember that depression doesn't discriminate, and it is really worth it for you to take the right steps to protect your mental health and make sure you don't burn out or cross over into depression.

Chapter 9

When History Repeats Itself

When 2015 rolled around, the year started off with me still being considered overqualified for the jobs I applied for. But on Friday, January 9, things took a turn for the better when I got an email from a private rehab facility, asking if I could come in for an interview the next week. I was so happy and grateful to receive that email, I felt in my gut that I was going to get this job! I had been emailing them since November, and we'd had a bit of a back-and-forth, and then I heard nothing from early December on, so I had given up on the idea of working at this beautiful facility or in a rehab anywhere in the province of Quebec, really.

It boggled my mind how many people in Los Angeles and Orange County were ready to hire me after having met me and seen firsthand what I could do during the Four-Day Relapse Prevention Counselling Training I'd attended in October 2014. If I hadn't been dating Mike and hadn't already had a hard time being away from him when I worked in the Dominican Republic, I would've been on the first flight to California the second I received the emails from those facilities interested in hiring me.

I'm not gonna lie—there were moments when I considered pausing our relationship so I could spread my wings and fly, but I'm grateful that I was a little more patient and stuck around to receive that email when I did, as I don't know if I would have been this blessed as I am with Mike in my life.

Needless to say, I got the job. I was so grateful to be given the opportunity to make a difference and put into practice what I had learned in all my years of training. I created different six-week programs and directly saw the benefits of them while running a couple group sessions a week at the centre (I have since recorded sessions and made them available to the public in the "Crush Your Unnecessary Suffering" program at alive316.com). Everything I teach in group coaching format to residents suffering from addiction and a comorbid mental illness, such as depression or even a personality disorder, is beneficial to anyone and everyone!

In most rehabs and counselling facilities in Quebec, burnout rates are high because there's usually a shortage of staff, and the workload becomes very demanding and draining. Although I was working in a private facility, it was still in its infancy, and it was not overstaffed by any stretch.

Working in addiction is tough, but in this case, it was even tougher because the criteria for admission to this specific rehab entailed having a comorbid psychiatric disorder. This means the patient would need to have primarily an addiction along with another mental illness. This automatically stepped up the challenge of working in a rehab, which I gladly accepted, at first. My self-care game wasn't top-notch at the time, so that didn't help, and my wanting to prove myself and get further in this field also didn't work to my advantage.

At around the six-month mark, a recruiter from an employee assistance company where I had once applied for an addiction counselling position reached out about a contract opportunity for me to offer consulting and counselling as an affiliate to their company. Essentially, I wouldn't be working for the company; they would just refer clients to me, and I could accept or reject the referral as I pleased. All I needed was an office to hold sessions in. Luckily, my manager at the rehab approved that during the time I was not seeing clients from the centre, I would be able to see the clients referred to me as part of the employee assistance program (EAP).

This allowed me to gain experience in another area of counselling and offer services in a more short-term format, using a solution-focused psychotherapeutic approach, which I had liked very much during my graduate studies and hadn't been given the opportunity to apply since graduating.

Given I felt myself burning out, I started subconsciously looking for an exit from the rehab centre, and that's probably why I was so ecstatic to hear from the recruiter of the other company, no matter how part time the offer was. By the seventh month, however, I started developing headaches more often and realized that for both my physical and mental health, I would have to call it quits at the rehab centre, so I did.

I gave a six-week notice of my departure, which is a long time for someone feeling physically and often mentally unwell, but when I knew my stay there was going to be temporary, a huge weight came off my shoulders, leading to a decrease in my headaches and sleep disturbance.

In the meantime, I looked into options for how I could continue to see clients referred to me from the EAP contract. Until the day I left the rehab, I saw them there, and then following this, I began to rent hourly space at the

Caplan Therapy Centre, and occasionally at my friend's counselling office downtown during the times he wasn't seeing clients.

This plan worked out, but I knew I wanted more. I wanted to have my own office space, as I had at the rehab centre, decorated the way I wanted and giving off the vibe I preferred. I believed the environment I was working in affected how I helped my clients, and so not long after, I began looking for my own office so I could officially go full swing into private practice.

I fell in love with the first place I landed on, which was the basement of an old home in Westmount. There were several other doctors, psychiatrists, and psychologists in the building, just as there were other professionals in the adjacent buildings (also old homes) on Sherbrooke Street, right across from Westmount Park. The furniture consisted of unique vintage and antique pieces that were very much my style, and I visualized hosting my clients the way I would host someone in my own home, with warmth and comfort.

I immediately said yes, comfortable that I would be able to make the rent, even with just the current clients I had from the contract, with the plan to build slowly from there.

Within ten days, I had secured two more contracts and then hired someone to start building my website so I could work on getting my own clients, outside of the EAP contract referrals. Part of the reason for this was that as much as those contracts were a blessing for getting me started on building my own practice, the hourly rate was nowhere near what my work was worth, and we would get paid up to forty-five business days after having completed the sessions the clients had been allocated. Again, a great way to start, but not a great way to maintain a steady income.

By October 10, I had my first office warming with family and relatives, as my office was big enough to fit about fifteen people. I could easily run counselling groups in a circle of up to ten, which was another reason I was so compelled to say yes when I saw the office. A couple days later, I held an office-warming party with friends as well. I was grateful for them having been there for me throughout my depressive episodes and for their support. We raised a glass of bubbly in my office and then went back to my parents' place for a lovely Momma Manarolis feast.

I was really excited for what was coming. I had recently attended a life coaching training and was excited to start including life coaching in my menu of services, as I'd noticed people were becoming more and more open to seeing a coach over a therapist.

I was grateful that I could offer both counselling and coaching, and for the endless possibilities that lay before me, especially after the experience I'd gained running groups in and out of the rehab centre. I had the space to run groups and workshops, and the office location itself added a bit of prestige, allowing me to attract a clientele that would be willing to pay me what I was worth.

All seemed well with the world and the direction I was headed in, minus how easily I could get distracted by my other passions, such as dancing with my troupe. An opportunity to perform on a TV show in Greece in the following month presented itself, and I couldn't help but say yes, pausing my professional momentum. It was not one of my wisest decisions (the TV show experience was really nothing to write home about), but overall, I enjoyed being in Greece in the fall. It allowed me to spend time with relatives who are typically unable to hang out during the busy high-summer season. They hadn't seen me since the summer of 2013 and wondered if my dating Mike had anything to do with it. I assured them it didn't, that it mostly had to do with adulting and building my career.

Then 2016 started off with a proposal in the middle of Las Vegas Boulevard while fireworks shot from the rooftops of five different hotels on the Strip, as the countdown for the New Year had just taken place. This is the kind of note the year began on, tears of joy and laughter, when I eventually said yes to Mike asking me to marry him.

***

The goal had initially been to hit the ground running as soon as 2016 started, to get my counselling and coaching business to the level I had anticipated before pausing the month before. I wanted to further my training as a coach and start offering my services virtually to people in different parts of the world. I wanted to network in Westmount and attend any event I could, to have conversations with the right people and get more clients as a result, the kind who would pay me then and there and not forty-five days later—the kind who were willing to invest in their personal development and enrichment.

Planning an engagement and a wedding and looking for a place to live was far from my 2016 radar when I'd set my annual goals. Since I'm five years older than Mike, he still had some of his own things he wanted to accomplish, so I honestly didn't expect a proposal that early on in our relationship. When I think back, I'm not sure why we were in such a hurry to plan a wedding so soon after he had proposed. There was no reason we couldn't delay or even move in together first. But excitement took over, and as happens with a fire sign such as me, when it does, things take their own course real quick.

Because I had been in Greece a little less than two months prior and had discussed hypothetical wedding dates with my relatives (apparently, I was putting a wedding out into the Universe when I decided to have those conversations), it had been determined that the only way any of them could make it to my wedding was if it took place in the winter, as all their businesses were summer establishments that operated in the Crete tourist season between April 1 and October 31. Somehow, this led us to decide that January 7, which is a pretty big holiday in the Greek Orthodox tradition, would be the ideal date. Christmas Eve 2016 fell on a Saturday, New Year's Eve fell the following Saturday, and the Saturday after that would be our wedding day!

Depression DOESN'T Discriminate

It seemed like an ideal scenario whereby anyone coming from Greece could do so over the course of the holidays, enjoy those, and then enjoy our wedding next. That, though, led to me having to focus on so much more than I had initially intended for 2016, and I was having a hard time with the idea of compromising my business goals for the year. So I pushed myself ... and pushed myself some more.

By October 2016, I started freaking out that if we kept the wedding date for January 7, I would be putting myself at risk of falling into another depressive episode. How had this even entered my mind? My brother and my mother had expressed their concerns to my personal trainer about my being prone to depression, and that by having a lot going on with the certificate I was trying to complete, my private practice, planning the wedding, planning a move, and the trainer's pressure to turn me into Fergie by the wedding day, perhaps I would sink again.

I felt myself burning out, and since I knew there was still a window of opportunity where I could change the date without losing any money and messing things up for people who were planning to travel, I acquiesced to changing the date. I felt a lot of guilt because I knew that moving the date to spring would mean I was eliminating the possibility of close relatives from Greece attending our wedding. Though I was sad and worried about my family members, it was not a reason to put myself at risk of deepening my burnout and developing depression again. Little did I know that moving the wedding by a little less than four months was still not enough time to preserve my sanity.

On January 8, 2017, I enjoyed an incredible bridal shower. My family managed to surprise me, which I appreciated very much as I love surprises, whether I'm the one doing the surprising or the one getting surprised.

Subconsciously, my need for significance has likely been behind my need to be surprised and/or to surprise others. When certain core needs are not met at critical periods of our lives, typically from birth to age eight, those needs very often drive our decisions and actions throughout our adult life. Unless we do the work and bring those unconscious needs to the forefront, they will continue to be what lies behind a lot of our emotions and actions and the direction we take in life. These needs are as much behind the bad decisions we make as they are behind the wonderful things we accomplish.

Bottom line, as a result of being the child of workaholic parents, some of my core needs were definitely not met, or not met enough, at least, and this has been behind a lot of my unhealthy behaviors.

We all prioritize our needs differently, and our decisions are based on which needs we put first. Once you learn to identify what those needs are and make conscious decisions about how to meet them, you can live a more aligned and healthy life, free of unnecessary suffering, such as anger, anxiety, and depression.

Don't get me wrong—I'm grateful my parents did everything they could to provide for us, and they modeled traits of persistence and determination that today are some of my best qualities. Work-life balance could have spared them so much grief, though, such as the wear and tear on their bodies and the emotional trauma they endured as a result of my major depressive episodes.

As a result of what I witnessed growing up, I adopted the art of pressuring myself. And clearly, I'd done a lot of that in 2016 and the first half of 2017 as I took on one major life transition after another, which is never a good idea, especially not for someone who is vulnerable to reexperiencing depression under periods of high stress. I thought I was done with depression, though, because I mistakenly believed that due to no longer having the learning difficulties I had struggled with most of my life, I was good to go.

Here's the thing—every life transition, however positive, is stressful! Yes, even adjusting to positive changes can cause stress, and the stress of change can be enough to induce mental health problems, such as anxiety and depression, for ANYONE, let alone someone with a history of depression. Stress actually drives us N.U.T.S.!

You read that correctly—N.U.T.S. is an acronym created by one of my McGill professors, Dr. Sonia Lupien, to explain the effects of stress in a nutshell. Essentially, the brain will release stress hormones if a situation is more than one of the following: **Novel, Unpredictable (and/or) Threatening**, either to your survival or your ego, and something over which you don't have a **sense of control.** You don't have to be working long hours or dealing with issues of life and death to feel stressed. It happens to us all, for a variety of reasons and especially during life transitions, given all four sources of stress are usually present.

Part of loving yourself authentically entails looking at the current stressors in your life, your unhealthy reactions to these stressors, as well as the unhealthy thought patterns that have taken over your brain. At the time, I didn't really love myself authentically, and as I have said time and time again on my livestreams and social media posts, a shortage of self-love is what nearly killed me, more than once.

***

So here I was in the first couple months of 2017, looking for a new apartment, furniture shopping, moving out of my parents' home, and moving into an apartment with Mike, while continuing to plan a big fat Greek wedding (it was more of a production, really), growing my private practice and my social media following on Instagram, planning a big honeymoon, taking classes, and still training for that "fit for life" body by my wedding.

All this during a harsh winter with little to no sunlight, while the EAP contracts consistently sent me clients suffering from depression. It's no secret that there is a difference in how much more taxing a session can be when a client comes to you with a diagnosis of depression versus coming to you for a workplace conflict they need resolved. To say I was exhausted leading up to my wedding is an understatement. I had no idea that I had begun experiencing burnout during that time and that stress was silently killing me.

In North America, most people experiencing burnout push through it because running on fumes has unfortunately been normalized over the years, if not celebrated. To top it all off, as 3:16 Day of 2017 approached, I was hard on myself for not having been more prepared to take this project much further. I put more pressure on myself to figure out what I was going to do on that day while already being overwhelmed with wedding-related details, keeping on top of the certification I was working toward, and catching up with client notes that I had fallen behind on.

I reluctantly accepted that I couldn't yet grow this movement to the level I wanted, given it was crunch time where the wedding was concerned. I had difficulty seeing it. It took my brother noticing how exhausted I was the night before 3:16 Day of that year to tell me that I needed to pace myself where the movement was concerned and that in due time, the movement would grow.

However, I was still trying to make it all work, almost as if I had forgotten what depression was like, even amid making it a point to let the world know I had survived it, along with my suicide attempt. There was a disconnect with what I was saying and preaching. Six years had gone by, and that episode, along with 3:16 Day, seemed like a distant memory. That didn't make me uneasy when I thought about it, almost as if it had never happened.

Tony and I created a short yet powerful video regarding why I post at 3:16 and why this day is so important to me. I was so tired after we finished, yet I still wanted to post it the next day, knowing there would be notifications left and right, even phone calls since a lot of people who knew me still had no idea I had attempted suicide six years prior.

Did I really need to add one more thing to my plate that would require me to give so much energy in the days that followed? Short and honest answer: NO. Was I oblivious to how bad things had gotten for my mental health by that point? Short and honest answer: also NO.

So, on March 16, 2017, six years after my suicide attempt, we released that one-minute video (now on its316andimalive.com). And I didn't just make one post, I made FIVE posts that day, to make sure as many people as possible would see it because I wouldn't be able to post or do much regarding this movement that I was so eager to progress.

Everything I predicted happened. The notifications nearly blew up my phone, and I answered every single comment, text, and call. Normalizing the conversation had officially reached another level, and this made my heart sing.

I lived off this high for a few days while in the grind of things. Then, exactly one month before the wedding, on March 29, I attended a Tony Robbins all-day event in Montreal. It was a "Power of Success" twelve-hour seminar, featuring multiple successful speakers to elevate us and promote their programs. Tony Robbins spoke for even longer than expected and offered life-altering advice (some of which I was already aware of because the last certification I was working on at the time was part of the Robbins-Madanes Training he offers).

I left that event feeling even higher, and the next day, I brought a very different energy into my sessions. I was also pumped to achieve my entrepreneurial goals and looking forward to my wedding and honeymoon being over with! Imagine that—I had worked so hard planning everything, and even though the events hadn't happened yet, I was already on to the next thing in my mind. A classic case of not really enjoying a journey and instead anticipating the final destination. Not helpful and not healthy either.

And still, I was finding ways to work on more things in the middle of crunch time, since I was concerned about losing my momentum from the Robbins' event, front row and up close and personal with Tony, someone I truly look up to.

Before I knew it, the week before my wedding had arrived, and only the close relatives who didn't run tourist season businesses had flown in. I decided to take that week off to greet them and tie up loose ends for the wedding day. Clearly, it wasn't really a week "off," given all the running around I had to do, but I didn't want to take longer than a week before the wedding as our honeymoon was scheduled to last three weeks. Factoring in that I would also need a couple days to recover, I did not want to take more than a total of five weeks off as I didn't like the idea of leaving my clients hanging for so long.

I remember feeling really tired that week and even begging my mom—yes, begging her—to cancel the Thursday night pre-wedding event she had planned. I was going to pick up the musicians from the airport that day, and we could've just had dinner with them at the house since they would be sleeping there, anyway. But no, my entire family insisted that it was tradition and that everything was going to run smoothly and I would take all day Friday to relax. My gut told me that wasn't going to be enough, as clearly my flame had started flickering long before that Thursday rolled around.

The Thursday night pre-wedding event happened, and yes, we had a really good time. I could barely sleep that night—from the excitement? From the hamster spinning on its wheel in my head? Was it a symptom of burnout? Most likely all of the above.

That Friday before my wedding, I was beyond exhausted when I went for my manicure and pedicure, followed by some last-minute wedding details. The morning of my wedding, while my favorite makeup artist was doing what she does best, I burst into tears. Someone had just said that Mike and the groomsmen were stuck in intense traffic, as Montreal had begun mass construction across the island. The men running that late meant we were not going to take photos where I'd wanted to, and that little add-on of stress sent me over the edge.

Bridesmaids and my mom started coming in as they heard I was crying, and my makeup artist told them I was emotional because of the day itself. I'm not sure to what extent she believed her own bullshit, but it was enough to get them out of the room so that I could stop crying and she could finish her artwork.

The wedding day didn't go off without a hitch, which was to be expected, given how many pieces there were to this production. The things that did go wrong were unexpected, and I felt very angry the next day and up until the day I boarded our flight to Dubai.

From an outsider's perspective, it was not only the wedding of the year but the wedding of the decade. That wasn't my perspective, though, as I had totally fixated on the things that were supposed to happen during my wedding that didn't, things that meant so much to me. I managed to start having a good time at my own wedding as of 1:45 a.m., when everything that was on the schedule for the evening had been completed and I no longer had to think of anything and could just let myself relax.

In retrospect, I can say that I would have very much benefitted from a wedding planner or at least a wedding coordinator that night, and since then I've done nothing but recommend this to future brides, especially those who consider planning something of the magnitude of our wedding.

At 1:45 a.m., I went to the bar and ordered two Malibu and pineapple cocktails, and that was the first time any alcohol entered my system that day. I literally chugged them one by one in front of the bartender and guests, and then ran up on stage to dance with my husband to some Oriental beats that my best friend played on his drum.

This "stress-free" time lasted until about 4:30 a.m., and with the night officially over, we walked to the McDonald's across the street. My husband and I had reserved the wedding suite at the hotel next door, so a little McDonald's run wouldn't delay us from sleeping. However, I didn't end up falling asleep until 7:00 a.m. and was wide awake by 7:45. This is how the first day of my marriage began—running on fumes.

We returned to the hall to tie up loose ends and carried on with other errands, then we gathered at my parents' home with all the other out-of-town guests and musicians who had flown in. Rest clearly continued to be off the menu.

In the next twenty-four hours, I ran around town and took care of post-wedding errands while packing for a nineteen-day honeymoon to two countries that were very different in style and weather—Dubai and Bali. I found myself thinking about what had gone wrong at the wedding and crying throughout the day.

Eventually, I got my shit together and we even went to the airport to send off the musicians, which was really not necessary but just one more thing I had a hard time saying no to.

The next day, it was our turn to fly out, and I kid you not, the obsession over what had gone wrong at the wedding continued to be very present, leading me to leave Montreal on a terrible foot. I remember my mom and brother being really concerned about me but also angry with the person who'd contributed to my wedding disappointment. They weren't scolding me for appearing ungrateful about how well everything else had gone, but they were totally feeding off my anger and agreeing with my major complaints.

Luckily, after we boarded the plane, Mike chose a movie, and I put on the audio version of a mindfulness book I'd wanted to read. Over the course of several hours, I found myself letting go and even forgiving the person I had been so infuriated with. I had Wi-Fi on the plane and made it a point to message my family to let them know I was way better than how I left them, and promised that we would have a fantabulous time on our honeymoon.

And we did just that.

The first six days of our honeymoon were in Dubai, the latter nine in Bali, and then we returned to Dubai for one more night. Rest, which is what I needed most, continued to evade me. When we got to Dubai, I did sleep more than usual, and at very odd hours, not having anything to do with the jet lag at that point. I recall my relative who lives in Dubai pointing out how there was something odd about how much I was sleeping in those first few days and the hours I was waking up. I didn't care; I just wanted to sleep some more, but I felt guilty about Mike not being able to do some of the things he wanted us to do in Dubai.

That right there was another indication of my running low on self-love. Despite my exhaustion, I was very much preoccupied with meeting someone else's needs, that of my husband. And unfortunately, this didn't end there.

I had been so looking forward to spending ten hours a day on a Bali beach, not realizing that my husband actually can't stand being at the beach for more than an hour. He has hardcore ADHD, feels restless when staying in one place too long where stimulation is lacking, and his eyes are sensitive to the sun. Who knew that I would marry someone who is the complete opposite of me where going to the beach—my happy place—is concerned?

On the first day, when Mike really wanted to go back to the room after an hour, I felt guilty for wanting to spend my days at the beach and reached out to one of my best friends in New York who had been to Bali on her honeymoon a couple months before, and who had recommended I hire a chauffeur to take us to all the wonderful sites Bali has to offer. And God knows there are many. I asked her for the name of the chauffeur she was pleased with and started making calls and plans, so I could make sure Mike would have the best honeymoon ever.

Here's the thing: Mike never asked me to leave the beach early, nor did he complain about my wanting to go to the beach. He expressed that he was more than happy to go back to the room and read some of the books he'd brought along, out of the sun and in a cooler environment. I am the one who made a bigger deal out of this than necessary, and I am the one who had a hard time establishing a compromise that would work for both of us. I was very much forgetting about what would be best for me at this point, as I guess the much needed vitamin D we'd been missing all winter had already started to boost my mood. Plus, getting a chauffeur for an entire day in Bali cost $50 USD, which was too good to pass up.

The roads in Bali are a mess, so I hired Jefta, and for five days out of that trip, he took us everywhere on that magical island.

I even remember my relatives in Dubai, who had visited Bali a few times over the last twenty years, telling me that we had done and seen more during those nine days than they had in all their trips combined. You can imagine that meant I was NOT returning to Montreal any more rested than I'd left.

When we returned home, I was exhausted and physically unwell, as I had contracted "Bali belly" toward the end of our trip, caused by consuming bacteria found in contaminated water. I had a lot of very uncomfortable cramping like nothing I'd ever experienced before. Readjusting to the eastern time zone also took its toll. This all pushed back my return to office by a couple more days, which made me feel worse about the delay in resuming client appointments.

When I got to my office several days later, I sat down at my desk, and something unusual happened. Whatever was on my desk, whatever files I had left incomplete the weeks before my wedding (and there were quite a few), whatever loose ends I needed to tie up on my return, it all felt insurmountable. Then I opened my work emails and saw an overdue notice—more like a warning at this point, since I had not responded to the notice the week of my wedding—regarding the Order of Guidance Counsellors (who I was licensed with) requesting to audit my files as part of an annual procedure they do to randomly selected members.

Right then, anxiety set in because I knew there was no way in hell I could prepare everything in time for an audit they were aiming to conduct in a few days.

I emailed them, in a panic, lying through my teeth about still being out of town, trying to buy myself time, and I started pushing through the anxiety at that moment. The next day, I resumed seeing clients, even while feeling very uneasy about my situation.

This went on for a few more days, and then on June 10, after completing a ninety-minute coaching session with a client, I noticed several missed calls from Mike and my mother-in-law. Already feeling so tired and numb, I called Mike back only for him to tell me that he'd been injured at work and that he'd been at the hospital for the last hour and a half.

I froze. I didn't know what to do. He told me he was OK, but that he sustained a nasty cut on his thumb and would likely need surgery, but they were unable to provide further details yet and I needed to get over there as soon as I was done with work.

Mike and I went home that night and then experienced another eleven stressful days as he absolutely needed surgery, but there were no rooms available. A surgeon was available, but an operating room was not, so we were on standby for eleven days, unable to go too far from the hospital radius in case we got called in for his surgery. That was beyond frustrating, and I didn't have much bandwidth left to allocate to more frustration. I stopped accepting new EAP referrals once I completed the sessions with other clients from those programs.

The surgery finally happened and ended up lasting three hours (instead of the promised thirty minutes) to repair what turned out to be a severed artery, tendon, and nerve. Waiting three hours for Mike to get out of surgery was very distressing, and it depleted me even more than I already was upon going into the hospital with him.

After Mike's discharge, he needed tending over the first few days. He also had difficulty sleeping in the position the doctor recommended and found himself moving around and waking me up a lot during the night. My sleep was pretty bad to begin with, so that certainly didn't help. The audit was scheduled to happen soon, and I was nervous as hell. It had taken so much to achieve the equivalency requirements (from my education outside Quebec) to be able to get this license to practice, so the idea of losing it was very anxiety provoking.

Every time my parents saw me, I was on edge. I didn't want to visit anymore as I was beyond tired after my sessions, most of which took place in the evenings, and I couldn't wait to get through the audit. It's as if I was only going to allow myself regular life activities after this potential audit finished. I didn't care to talk to or see anyone else at that point, and even dealing with Mike, who was scared of never regaining full function of his thumb, which would render him unable to move forward in his cooking career, had become too much.

Recovering from an injury or a surgery that nearly cost someone their livelihood can be a challenging and emotional experience. Depending on the nature and severity of the surgery, one may have to face a long and difficult road to recovery, which may include physical pain, fatigue, and difficulty with everyday tasks. The added financial stress and uncertainty that comes with not being able to work during the recovery period surely doesn't help.

All of this is what Mike experienced at that point. His mental and emotional well-being were undoubtedly affected. I noticed him feeling overwhelmed and distressed about his situation, and by that point, I also found myself more distressed, given I would have to pay our steep rent on top of my office rent.

Mike was worried about how he would support us and when he would be able to do so again, and I was worried about how I was going to support us if the audit of my files went south. He was frustrated and discouraged by not being able to return to his normal routine, and I was frustrated beyond measure about both our routines being disrupted. Nowhere in all this did I show empathy or understanding. I was so depleted and consumed by my own shit that I failed to show the love of my life that everything was going to be all right.

It's important for someone in this kind of predicament to have a strong support system, whether it's family, friends, or a support group, and to consider getting counselling or coaching to cope with the stress of the entire situation. Unfortunately for Mike at that point, the person he was living with wasn't the ideal support, as I wasn't patient nor a beacon of hope for him. It had become evident (and confusing to him) that I would provide a poor contribution to his recovery; I barely wanted to be around him, and he could tell.

Mike wasn't imagining things, as others, including my mom, had confirmed noticing that I wasn't at my most pleasant around him, or anyone really. And honestly, I don't recall how I ended up accepting to go for lunch with him just a couple days before the audit, but I did, and we even ended up having a huge and unnecessary argument, asking for the check way sooner than we normally would. After this short and very unpleasant lunch in Westmount, we coldly walked back to our apartment together. I rushed out of the elevator without him and upon reaching our door, I had to slow down to dig deep in my purse for my keys. By the time I inserted the key into the keyhole, he had caught up to me, and as I turned the key to the right, Mike asked,

"Sophs…

Do you think you might be depressed?"

Epilogue

I believe that self-love is an ongoing conscious choice that each and every one of us <u>can</u> make and that is absolutely worth making.

Why?

Because as you now know, making the opposite choice nearly killed me.

A shortage of self-love is really what led to burn out. A shortage of self-love led me to push through that burnout and develop a brutal episode of major depression that led me to nearly end my life more than once.

By now, I hope you believe me when I tell you that depression **DOESN'T** discriminate. This unseen *monster* can happen to any one of us, no matter how well life appears to be going.

The good news is, learning how to love yourself can not only transform your life but it can save it.

I believe I'm still here because my purpose is to prevent as many people as possible from having to experience what I did, to prevent **you** from ever having to experience that, and to teach *you* how to love yourself, like your life depends on it. Because it DOES.

As I wrote this book, the project developed into something greater than I could've ever imagined. Visit (www.316epilogue.com) to watch a short video about what the experience of writing this book was like and on what's coming up next in Part 2, *The Monster Strikes Back*.

About The Author

Sophia Manarolis, M.Ed., is a real human being, one with scars and vulnerability coupled with a fearlessness to be authentic and speak her truth. She is not only someone who has survived major depression and multiple suicide attempts, she is a mental health advocate often referred to as a mental health warrior.

Manarolis combines her experience overcoming depression and suicide attempts with her master's level training in counselling and her training as a certified life coach to help her clients feel lighter, freer, and more alive. She spearheads a global movement dedicated to preventing people from enduring the unnecessary suffering that leads to burnout and depression.

Furthermore, she believes that together through **#its316andimalive**, we can normalize the conversation surrounding depression so those suffering in silence know that they never have to fight alone ever again.

As she commonly states, "Life is too short to be and feel anything else but ALIVE."

Made in the USA
Columbia, SC
12 September 2023

9e8ba454-5078-4040-86db-8f329a58c2d1R02